One in a Million

A True Story by Miriam

Miriam Hodges, Author
and
Holly Rubin Sills, Co-Author and Editor

One in a Million
A True Story by Miriam

Copyright, 2015
Miriam Hodges
Holly Rubin Sills

All Rights Reserved

No text or images in this book
may be used or reproduced in any
manner without written permission
of the copyright holders.

Printed in the United States of America

ISBN: 978-0-9759533-8-9

Published by
Legacies & Memories
St. Augustine, Florida

(888) 862-2754
www.LegaciesandMemoriesPublishing.com

Contents

Chapter 1   11
The People's War of 1939
    Churchill and the "Haunting of Dunkirk"
    Children of War

Chapter 2   17
Miriam of Nottingham
    Singing and Dancing at Four
    The Voluntary Entertainment Service

Chapter 3   23
It's Raining Men
    The Attraction of an Officer in Uniform
    My First Love, William Brown
    Dating

Chapter 4   29
The One and Only "Jack Hodges"
    April 1945: Jack's Proposal
    Marry Me TOMORROW
    Married and Still Entertaining

Chapter 5   37
Making My Way to Jack
    Salisbury Processing Camp
    Miriam Sails to America on the Queen Mary
    Meeting Jack in New York Harbor

Chapter 6   43
Life with Jack in America
    Working in America
    Mother and Father's First Trip to America
    1948: Back to England

Chapter 7 — 49
Entertaining in our New Home
    Too Coincidental – Friends for a Lifetime
    After Five; Fun & Fabulous Festivities

Chapter 8 — 55
Sylvia, Mark and Meaningful Memories
    Pool Time Activities
    The Birth of Mark
    Father and Mother Return to America

Chapter 9 — 63
Miriam's Memorable Voyage
    Meeting James Andrew
    1950's Travel Highlights
    Responsibilities of the Heart
    My Father – John William Green

Chapter 10 — 69
Life's Decisions and Celebrations
    A New Business Opportunity
    Our Roger

Chapter 11 — 75
A Vacation Home & Holiday Memories
    Our Condo at the Racquet Club
    Remembering the Holidays as a Child
    Christmas Time and "The Ship of Fools"

Chapter 12 — 79
40 Years of Wonderful Memories
    Our 40th Wedding Anniversary
    The "Joy" of My Sister Joyce
    My Sister Kathleen

Chapter 13   87
The 70's & 80's
    Grooving in the 70's
    1982: Jack's Retirement
    Moving to Florida Full-Time
    Disney World, USA

Chapter 14   93
1986: Our New Home in the Galleons
    New Friends and More Pleasure
    Golf & Tennis
    Planes and Boats – What Fun!

Chapter 15   101
Amazing Journeys
    Puerto Rico & Acapulco
    Our California Road Trip
    Maine and Canada

Chapter 16   111
The Rotary Club
    The Rotary Club of Virginia
    Vero Beach Rotary
    International Rotary Convention – France

Chapter 17   117
The Love in My Heart
    My Mother
    My Forever Jack

Preface

As she sips from her cup of tea looking out at the Atlantic Ocean, Miriam Hodges shares her exuberant life stories in a quietly confident yet selfless and stylish manner. And it was through her charming English accent that I began to learn about her clever and creative side, which she developed as a child in Nottingham England.

Then in 1939, when Britain declared war on Germany, Miriam's exuberance for life did not waiver. And during a historical upheaval in time, she found a positive purpose by entertaining British and American troops with her father on stage through song, dance and comedy.

Her knack of turning comical and engaging situations into a form of spicy romance demonstrated her sense of self, which became all the more captivating to all she would meet. And then through the power of attraction, she met that "one in a million" special man named Jack Hodges, who convinced her to commit her heart and soul into love, step by step.

After a turbulent and emotional transatlantic crossing to America and leaving her family in England, Miriam's life with Jack began to unfold into an illuminating lifestyle filled with meaningful people and an insightful journey.

Not often can someone share those intimate times in life, but Miriam did. This British woman is not just any woman. She is fascinating and extraordinary and with her husband Jack by her side, they were able to create a lifetime of friends from around the globe, through hours of chatting, entertainment and laughter. And through the depth of her strength, courage and magical personality, Miriam shares a series of energized and personal happenings that are full of moving examples of how important finding that "one in a million" can make all the difference in creating a lifetime of happiness.

Holly Rubin Sills, Co-Author and Editor

One in a Million

A True Story by Miriam

Chapter 1
The People's War of 1939

This earth, this realm, this land of hope and glory, this mother of the free, is the land we know today as the Kingdom of England. While once ruled by Rome, it is the one and only England I came to love and know. On September third 1939, Britain declared war on Germany and Prime Minister Chamberlain was completely devastated. His peace talks with Berlin had failed and his final words were heart wrenching, "I trust I may live to see Hitlerism destroyed". The next day the British Royal Air Force launched its first bombing mission against Germany and within a week many convoys would begin to cross Atlantic waters. By September 17th, Britain's first air craft carrier was sunk and almost immediately the British and French empires joined in turning it into a worldwide war, fought not only in Europe, but across the great ocean.

Nottingham was the first city in Britain to build an air raid notification system and numerous public shelters. On May 8th and 9th of 1940, over 100 bombers were in the Nottingham raid. Others would follow. We were all issued gas masks and assigned to the local Anderson Bomb Shelter, which was located at the top of the garden area where we lived. The size was only large enough for a big dog, so we were all very cramped. We could not even think clearly, as it was all so devastating. Frightened and fearing for our lives, we asked ourselves "Would we ever survive?"

Shortly after that, France surrendered on June 17th 1940, and pictures of Hitler dancing in the streets filled the newspapers after he was told Paris had fallen. To see the German troops marching past the Arc de Triomphe in Paris was terrifying, and many of us stood quietly in the shadows of the darkness. And every evening the bombs would target certain towns, and the skies would light up with clouds of smoke and streaks of bright lights. The loud air raid sirens would sound off in the middle of the night, a signal for us to find safety and take cover.

Father determined the local shelter was not the best place for us, so he decided to make our coal cellar the sleeping quarters for our family. He shoveled the coal to one side and placed sleeping cots on the other. But the conditions were very also poor in the cellar, and after about a week we decided to take our chances, and moved back into our own beds in the main house.

Every night we would hear our Britain's Lancaster Bombers fly over our house, and every morning we would eagerly wake to turn on the radio only to hear the news of missing planes, never to return. Early on in the war the pilots were mostly British, but then the Canadians, the Polish, and the Turks all collaborated together for one final cause. So many missions were implemented, with barely any rest for the pilots in between. Little did they know hundreds of these brave men would save England by becoming a much stronger force in the air. You see, they were fooled, but not without significant cost for many families who lost their loved ones. Oh how pitiful it was that all of these young men lost their lives to protect us. It was all such an enormous waste, resulting in the unnecessary loss of valuable human lives.

Yes, it was the people's war, and Germany was out to destroy us. London was the hardest hit, then Coventry, Liverpool and Hull. The people in London used the underground tunnels for cover, and such bravery was displayed by all. Everyone would help each other, while sharing what little they had. "Would you like a half of my sandwich or a cup of soup?" one said. "A cup of tea for you miss?" No matter what they had, everyone found comfort in each other. Even a little music, a few songs to make the time go by, anything to try and keep hope together and fears far apart. Then, just as the "all clear" sounded off, everyone would run outside to the shock of seeing their homes destroyed, gone...and more lives lost, many buried in the rubble. The sadness echoed throughout the thick air and the tears were difficult to hold back. Can you imagine all the brave soldiers fighting, only to return to this disaster? Hitler thought he could break our spirit, but obviously he did not know the British.

King George VI and Queen Elizabeth stayed in London, which was very noble and advantageous for the people's morale. They were there to give everyone courage and support, even doing their part by visiting bombsites to pull everyone back together. Elizabeth, their daughter, became a driver with the ATS (Auxiliary Territorial Service), which was the women's branch of the British Army. She demonstrated great personal courage to help others, which inspired many. Later, more women were recruited for several different positions, same as the men, including the Women's Auxiliary Air Force (WAAF), and the WRENS (Women's Royal Navy Service) and even the Land Army. Other people, in general, continued to work on the farms or in the factories, demonstrating a superb effort to keep everyone operating together toward one common goal.

Churchill and the "Haunting of Dunkirk"

While the war in 1940 was terrifying, Dunkirk haunted the world. It was in June when the allied forces of Dunkirk located on the Belgium coast ended, and German forces captured the beach port. From May 26th till June 4^{th,} the German movement had virtually pinned all the British expeditionary forces against the sea. Rescue operations begun immediately in England, and a motley fleet of war ships, tugs, yachts and small craft set out, and hundreds of civilians, went to the rescue. Some of the boats could hardly make it; oh such courage. Within ten days, more than three hundred and forty British and French soldiers were lost, including two hundred and thirty five ships. Later, two other French ports on the English Channel were linked to Dunkirk, synonyms for heroism against terrible odds.

Two years later in March of 1942, Operation Chariot implemented an audacious combined raid on the port of Saint Nazaire, in German occupied France. Allied commandos deprived the Germans of repair facilities for their battleships, and a largely Canadian force was cut in half on a reconnaissance in force. United soldiers were trapped between the Germans and the channel, and they were firing hopelessly with rifles at the German planes. Some were taken off the beaches by small craft, and some ferried out to larger ships. Such dreadful times; I suppose it is best resembled in an old movie called "Mrs. Miniver", a classic World War II melodrama that won seven Oscars, and portrays that heroic war story that many of us will never forget.

I have always admired the English in how they would come to the rescue, no matter how young or old, no matter how aged the boats were; they were always there to help. It is hard to praise any one man, when there were so many that were fearless and valiant. Miracles came from all around, especially those from Winston Churchill. He was truly our rock, our strength.

On May 10th. 1940 at six in the evening, King George summoned Churchill to Buckingham Palace and told him, "I want you to form a government". At this time Churchill was the first Lord of the admiralty, and suddenly his entire life came into focus. It was as if everything he had done, everything he had known, his failures and frustrations, but no less than his achievements, were all contrived to aim him for this one great task - the Prime Minister of Britain. Now he had to hold firm to his convictions when common sense of the instants were against him. He would need to take on supportable burdens of work. Winston Churchill was one of the greatest and most proficient leaders of the twentieth century, if not of all time.

History tells us about Winston Churchill's beautiful mother named Jennie Jerome. She was an American, and his father was Lord Randolph Churchill. On the night of November 30th, 1874, Churchill's soon to be mother "Jennie" was gracefully waltzing across the ballroom floor at Blenheim Palace, when she felt labor pains two months ahead of time. She was immediately taken to the cloakroom, and surrounded by the wraps of all the guests and a flurry of excited women. On that night, Winston Leonard Spencer Churchill was born and he adored his mother. He was an amazing man and could exist on only four hours of sleep a night. He loved his brandy and cigars, and became a loyal friend of President Roosevelt. He had one daughter named Sarah, who went on stage and made a movie with Fred Astaire called "Royal Wedding". With all that Churchill gave to us, and all of those years of service; we should be ashamed of how badly we repaid him. We should be grateful. Without him, I truly wonder if we would have even won the war. Later in life, I was so pleased to go to Blenheim Palace to see all of his accomplishments and memories.

Children of War

When the war was declared, all the children were evacuated, many were taken away from their families and loved ones, tearing many close families apart. Imagine seeing your children taken away from you, and a tag placed on their clothing to take them to a safe place. And parents did not know if they would ever see their own children or family members again. They were all being sent to different parts of England, Scotland and overseas to Canada and America. Then we heard on the radio some horrific news. Many of the boats carrying the children were torpedoed and they were all lost at sea. How could anything be more devastating? But it didn't end there

As I reminisce, I feel such a conflict inside my heart of both good and bad circumstances that came from the war. There were so many kind people who opened their homes and hearts to those particular children, who finally did make it to safety. These new families became so fond of them, and treated them as if they were their own offspring. But sadly, most of the children were sent away for as long as five years, with their parents missing the most important part of their growth and development. Then when the children returned, there were various adjustments that had to be made. Some children had become accustom to a "well to do" life abroad, which was very different than back home in Nottingham. Many other children and families did not have it so well, and numerous downhearted stories were told and lost in those days. I just wish more information had been shared about those rare and exclusive times. Oh and yes, there were some mothers who could not part with their children at all, and took all the risks of not sending them away. That was an enormous decision and responsibility for many mothers during those times. And when the war was over, it became especially difficult for all the service men to return home as the head of their household, only to be seen as a stranger by their children. You can imagine the challenges of a different nature this presented, especially when the occasion of discipline occurred. But over time, things seemed to settle down and fall in place.

Chapter 2
Miriam of Nottingham

Before I venture further, I suppose this is as good of time as any to formally introduce myself. I am Miriam, the youngest of three daughters' born to John and Sarah Green, known as Sally and Jonnie from Nottingham, England. Our town was famous for Robin Hood, Sherwood Forest, Sheriff of Nottingham, the Castle and handmade luxury Nottingham lace, just to name a few. A statue of Robin Hood still stands in the castle grounds, complete with bow and arrow which has been known to be frequently stolen. One of my favorite places in Sherwood Forest was always the colossal Major Oak Tree. It is thirty three feet wide, and ninety two feet tall, and known as the oldest oak tree in Britain; estimated at over 1000 years old. But that's not the only reason it is so popular. It is also said to be where Robin Hood's merry men took shelter, and seats are carved out all around the tree for his men. Did Robin really exist? Well I am not going to give that up, but we all know it has made an excellent story for tall tales and great movies!

Singing and Dancing at Four

I was the last child to be born and had heard I was a mistake. But, I turned out to be mother's best friend and helper growing up. In later years we became even closer,

Miriam as a child.

and I was able to give both my mother and father a lot of loving care. At the age of four years old, with blonde curls, lots of confidence and a talent to sing and dance, my mother put me on stage. We all know how young children can steal a show. Well, that certainly happened to me, and it continued to impact my life from that point forward.

Not too far from where I lived was an all-girls school in England, close enough to ride my bicycle. All the girls had to wear a uniform, which I thought was great because we didn't have to compete on how each of us dressed. I remember the nice navy blue blazer we wore with a shiny crest on the lapel. But I have to admit, the required black stockings were just not my style.

The Voluntary Entertainment Service

At fifteen years of age, I left school and joined the V.E.S. (Voluntary Entertainment Service), which was a talent show created by my father for servicemen.

I had a dear friend named Irene, who also joined me on stage. She was two years older than I, but we had known each other since I was six. Irene and I went everywhere together, and we had so much fun singing and dancing in concert. One of our favorite songs that we danced to was the "Chattanooga Choo-Choo", which was written and produced in 1941, originally by the Glenn Miller Orchestra. Oh…. how I loved to sing and dance.

Father continued to put us on stage to make the servicemen laugh and smile. No matter the language they spoke, they all had the same reaction, which became very inspiring and motivating for me. I have to admit, I did have good legs and the sexy costumes were just part of our show for either dancing, singing or used as part of the background. The officers who sat in the front row were the ones we poked the most fun at, and played games with. Irene and I would always pick on the one I fancied the most.

At sixteen I was quite mature for my age, and on occasion we would invite a couple of officers on a date, then bring them to one of our homes after the show. On other occasions after the show, we would meet officers in the mess hall, and were regularly treated to Italian pastries created by chefs that were interns. They were so tasty that if I had been able to, I would have taken them home, but doggy bags had not been created yet.

The singing and dancing we presented to the armed forces felt amazing in so many ways, but it was also heartbreaking. As I was dancing on stage, I noticed many badly burned pilots; a site I certainly will never forget. I often asked myself; "How could these brave men face their life with being so disfigured?" I admired their courage and strength to continue on in life; something that became a very humbling lesson for me.

By that time, father had me dancing and singing on stage regularly and joining his sophisticated British classic comedy act called, "Wit and It". I played the dumb blonde and father portrayed my stage partner. He was handsome and young enough looking, so it worked out well, and we became a huge success. My father was a great man and taught me many things. I truly admired him. The song "Oh Johnny" was very popular back then and was ideal for our performance. I learned quickly how to dance to the beat of the music and ad lib whenever needed. The song itself makes sad hearts jump for joy, so I performed based on the words, and moved my body rhythmically to the music, improvising my steps and gestures accordingly.

Over time I improved my singing skills, and developed a very good soprano voice. I also became a talented dancer and very knowledgeable in choreographing performances. Everyone worked together as a team, and many of us were active with all aspects of the show. Finally, I became good enough for solo acts. I sang to songs like "Don't Sit under the Apple Tree", while twirling and swaying across the stage with a large smile on my face. I really enjoyed those days and even more important, making a positive difference to all the troops in the audience.

Our shows became more and more popular, and father and I became well known on stage. We also had requests to travel to different locations where many troops were located; some in very isolated places and a bit more dangerous. All of us had a concerned feeling when we took the show on the road, but we were needed and we weren't going to say "no". Then it happened...... one night we barely escaped death. Right in the middle of our performance the commanding officer ordered us from the back of the room yelling, "Stop the show! Get your people out of here right now! Go into the Grand Hall, and hurry!" We immediately stopped performing and rushed out, boarding a large bus outside. We were all told to lay flat on the floor. Then all of a sudden we heard an incredibly loud explosion. The Grand Hall had taken a direct hit, and the blast was substantial. We had just fled in time, thanks to Navy Intelligence. Trembling all over, we looked at each other, and with tears in our eyes we said a little prayer of thanks, and just wanted to go home.

But the shows had to go on, and were continued after our near death experience. We were given extra clothing coupons, in order to buy evening dresses and costumes to recreate our troop shows all over again. And this time the acts were even better. We added some very talented individuals, including one man playing the violin with his feet, then two violins at the same time. Another was an act with three boys who played xylophones, and the camaraderie we developed was just like one close happy family. We included very good opera singers, and I heard "One Fine Day" from Madam Butterfly, many times. I so loved that song as it was so joyful, but occasionally ended in me almost sobbing. I became so fond of entertaining. I guess it was just in my blood. It is true, there is no business like show business.

During the lunchtime hour we produced a very popular live broadcast on the radio called "Workers Playtime," for all factory workers. The troop entertainment took place all during the war and continued after it ended on May 8th, 1945 and ran into early August. In 1946, I was so delighted to receive a personal recognition letter from the President of the Voluntary Entertainment

Miriam ready for stage.

Services Northern Command Unit, and the Nottingham Association of Artists for Entertaining Troops. It thanked me for being a member of the "Aristocrats" Concert Party, and for giving pleasure to many thousands of "His Majesty's Forces", who were stationed in and around the city during World War II. It is a letter of distinguished honor and I am very proud of to this very day.

Chapter 3
It's Raining Men

The Attraction of an Officer in Uniform
    I met lots of men during those years. Most had attended the show and waited to meet me at the end. Being on stage in front of all of them was very gratifying, in more ways than one. There were so many good looking brave men, I couldn't help but keep a constant smile on my face. Just seeing all of them in uniform truly signified a level of power, stability and honor-wow! Their uniforms particularly intrigued me. No matter the color or style, I found myself especially attracted to the officers, and the pilots were my biggest weakness.
    In 1944 President Eisenhower came to England and visited Nottingham to introduce the "Eisenhower Battle Jacket," which was a stunning olive green color. Oh my! Eisenhower was so handsome in his uniform. I distinctly remember all the different jackets and uniforms the men wore, especially because I could see them all from the stage. Any ordinary looking man truly looked like a movie star, dressed in uniform with all their striking, different and honorable attire. The American officers' uniform was fantastic, and called the "Pink and Greens". The English paratrooper officers' uniform was truly detectable, especially when they sported their grass green or golden tan uniforms with red berets.

James Brown from Canada: Miriam's first love.

Oh, and the Navy officers looked very sharp donning a prominent gold braid, along with gold color buttons on their dinner dress whites or dinner dress blues. Army officers particularly stood out with their hats, matching brown belts and colors varying from blue to green to white with gold piping down the legs. I have to confess, seeing an officer in uniform was that kind of "knight in shining armor" feeling that really worked for me.

My First Love – William Brown

In 1942 and at the age of 17, I fell in love with a wonderful Canadian pilot named William James Brown from Victoria, British Columbia. Bill was so loving, good looking, kind and fun. And when he wasn't flying and could get away from the base, he would be at my house. If I was doing a show, he would join my family at home and wait for me. My sisters were only too happy to entertain him. The family knew he was very special to me. We spent a wonderful weekend in London, but not without mother and father's approval, because they trusted him immensely. But you must know that we did not sleep together, which I know is unheard of in this day and age. Instead, we spent wonderful evenings, dancing occasionally at the Strand Palace Hotel in central London. And after dinner he would shower me with cuddles and kisses. We were both so happy to be together, enjoying every single moment and doing our best to forget about the war.

Bill flew Lancaster Bombers, which were used by the Royal and Canadian Air Force. Life was good and we were in bliss, but sadly it did not last long. I was informed by his friend Jimmy Dillon, that Bill had been killed on a bombing raid, but wanted me to know how much I meant to him. We had two unforgettable months together that will never be forgotten. As time went on, I continued to be in despair, expecting to see him around every corner. It was so difficult…. I could not believe I wouldn't see him again. You always remember your first love. He was only 22 years old when his life ended. How awful it was for his family to lose such a wonderful son and for me to lose my first love. War was truly hell.

Jimmy Dillon became a good friend of mine and loved being with our family. He was an American pilot and had flown before the war, then joined the Canadian Air Force as an American, but not yet in the war. Jimmy and I had no romance, as I still was missing Bill. Jimmy had taken a lot of Bill's belongings after he passed away, and placed them in mother's kitchen cabinets, including some of his personal things like camera's etc. Then another heart wrenching loss; Jimmy was killed one month later, shared with me once more by a friend. I was so down, and it became more obvious that pilots did not stand a chance in the early war years.

After Bill and Jimmy were gone, I tried to go on a couple of dates, but it was truly a time of grief. I started to find some solace in being with my girlfriend Irene. I was 18 and Irene 20, and it wasn't long before I started to feel that a bit better and realized I needed to move beyond my loss of Bill.

Dating

  Much time had passed and it was time to incorporate some "fun activities" into my misery. So, Irene and I started to create some diversions and unscrupulous fun with some of the other servicemen. The Australian and New Zealander men were very tall and I was quite small; only five foot high, so I literally had to look up to them. That in itself was fun.

  One time we organized a double date with two Paratroop Platoon officers. They wined and dined us at their hotel, expecting us to spend the night. At the right moment we made a fast exit, which was a very narrow escape, and we laughed our way all the way home. Another time I was at the Palais, a great place to dance to Glen Miller type of music. It was there I noticed all the girl's swooning over another terribly handsome pilot officer. As I stood on the sideline and watched, he turned around and came up to me and asked me to dance. Why he asked ME to dance I don't know, but as he held me in his arms and pulled me close to his chest, he asked if I would sleep with him that night. I said "yes", so he never left my side for the rest of the evening. I was the envy of all the girls wondering why I was so special. The dancing was almost over for the evening, then the band began to play "Goodnight Sweetheart" as their final song. As everyone began to leave, I dashed to get my coat and made another quick getaway. I am sure it was not long before I was replaced, but I had so much fun and many lessons learned.

  Apart from the sadness of what was happening with the war, I found myself grateful and delighted to be young and part of everything, especially around so many men. Mother was a big help in managing all the attention I was getting. She would let one man through the front door, while I was letting a different one out the back. She loved the attention too, and we both enjoyed those distinct, unique and special times together.

I dated only two English officers; one I might have married after the war, the other one was a disaster. He even took me to meet his mother, but I was so busy with the troop shows I couldn't pay him enough notice. I also met a very nice officer from Sydney Australia, but that didn't last either, because he liked me too much and I did not feel the same way about him.

After many boyfriends, my girlfriend Irene met a Canadian Pilot named Lee Evans, and it was beautiful to see them so blissful and content together. They later married and I was her bridesmaid. Lee had someone he wanted me to meet, so the four of us could go on a date together. He introduced me to Frank, a past Ice Hockey player before the war, and a pilot from Saskatchewan, Canada. We had so much fun and he had a great deal of charm. We became engaged, but only after he broke his original engagement with his girlfriend back in Canada. Frank's last name was "Chad", and mother had said his name must have been shortened. She was right. It turned out he had a long polish name, and father did not feel he was the right man for me. Frank and I would fight a lot, and one time I even threw his clothes right out the window, but he always came running back. One night when I thought Frank was on duty, I decided to go out dancing with a girlfriend. While dancing with another attractive officer, Frank appeared and I introduced him as my fiancée. Frank garishly said, "ex-fiancée" and walked out. That was the end of that relationship, and my family was very pleased. I realized I had been saved from a big mistake, not to mention I would have hated that part of Canada. In addition, Lee later told me Frank had been married three times and had thirteen children. How lucky was I to abscond from that!

Shortly after my relationship ended with Frank, I met Max, a young Canadian officer who was in the mess hall after the show. A pilot of course; very young and handsome and hopelessly in love with me. It was his first time, and after that evening he came to see me every time he was in Nottingham. We had lovely times together, and he was quite sure I would be his wife. But after two months, I received a letter from him. It proceeded to tell me how much he loved me, and asked me to please write his parents, if anything should ever happen to him. He also wanted me to thank them for him, and to share with them all about us. He wrote in his letter that he would have been in to see me that night, but could not leave the base. He asked that I not flirt with any other man while I was doing the troop shows, and wanted me to remember that I was his and his alone. Two nights later, a colleague of his approached me and said that Max had been killed in a bombing raid. I was saddened once more. He was so young, and I felt horrible he would never have a life. My only consolation was that I knew he had experienced "love" at the end of his life. I was happy that at least I gave that to Max. Mother was very sad for me and wished I would not bring home anymore pilots. That was going to be difficult.

Chapter 4
The One and Only "Jack Hodges"

Then I met Jack Hodges, an American pilot with the ninth Air Force stationed at Cottesmore, England. Jack was an officer and a real Virginia gentleman. When I brought Jack home, he would sit by the fire with mother. She loved him and he won her over fast. Mother even gave him a "tea cozy" to keep his feet warm, and the smile on his face was priceless. It was November and Jack was always cold - so hard for him to get used to the dampness in England. Jack shared many stories with me, and some included his good friend Fred, who was a wrestler before the war. When Jack was in France, they would get together and often share many humorous stories. I was glad he had different buddies to share with. Jack would always wait for me to come home from the shows, and sometimes would manage to borrow a jeep from his base to come and see me.

When Jack and I first met, I had just started to see another pilot from Kentucky, but Jack soon took care of that. Jack also was dating a WREN, but terminated that once he realized he only wanted me. He was 24 years old and had several girlfriends back home, and one in particular that his mother wanted him to marry. But from that point on, we did not date anyone else and had very little time together, making each moment extra special.

April 1945 – Jack's Proposal

In April of 1945 and at 19 years old, Jack asked me to marry him. I was not sure what I really wanted, but I said "yes" thinking I could get out of it, if need be. Jack was very sure I was the one for him and he really loved me. He proposed to me during lunch at the Black Boy Hotel, located in Nottingham. The next step was for Jack to ask my father, so he took him to a local pub to bring up the subject. Father really liked Jack, but he did not like the idea of losing a daughter. It would mean breaking up our show, which was very well known and extremely popular. Father was also concerned that I would be going to a strange country, but felt certain Jack would be a good husband and take the best of care of me. Nonetheless, I was very young, quite spoiled -especially men wise - from being on stage in front of all the troops. But Jack won father over and he finally gave his approval.

The date of our wedding was set for May 17th. It was to be a church wedding with all the trimmings. My dress had to be made along with my sister's Joyce and my best friend, who was my bride's maid. Father was to give me away, and mother planned the reception and the invitations were sent. During this time before the wedding, Jack had to return to France.

On the night of May the 7th, while Jack was having a drink in the officer's mess hall, the Aerodrome officer came to him. He said, "Hodges, aren't you supposed to get married on the seventeenth?" "What do you mean supposed to?" Jack said, "Everything is arranged and I already have my pass to go over there." "Well, I am not supposed to tell you, but tomorrow is V.E. day (Victory in Europe), and the war is over. We are all being shipped to Trinidad." "WHAT?" Jack said in a state of shock. He immediately went to the commanding officer and told him his sad story. What a blessing that the commanding officer *also* had a British girlfriend. The commander told Jack there was a courier leaving for Kettering, and if he could be back in time, then he could fly back over to get married. Jack even managed to bring his good friend

Bert Utis, back to Nottingham with him. This was great for Jack because he was a nervous wreck, and Bert would help him through it all. Bert was very nice-looking and made a fine best man for the wedding. How they ever managed to get to Nottingham was a miracle. They even lucked into a train.

Before Jack left the base, the Padre wanted to talk with him. He said to Jack, "You will have to be the father, the mother, a sister and brother to your new bride. She is leaving her family to be in a strange country with a man she hardly knows. You have to be kind, patient and give ninety percent of yourself, while giving her your time and lots of loving care". What a godsend Padre was, and Jack never forgot his words and certainly not his advice.

Marry Me TOMORROW

It was May the 8th when Jack arrived on my doorstep, and I could tell that something was wrong. I could not believe it when he said to me, "Miriam, we have to get married TOMORROW!" Miriam's family asked Jack to please wait to get married, but Jack said, "No, Miriam will not be here", and I think he was right. Who knows how long it would have taken him to get back to England. By this time, news of the end of the war had circulated and everyone was celebrating. How could Jack and I possibly find someone to marry us on such short notice? Thanks to father, he had a friend who was a registrar and kind enough to marry us at the registry office in Nottingham. What a mad rush.

Now it was the morning of May the 9th, and Jack stopped by the florist insisting he needed flowers right away. Since I did not have my wedding dress yet, I got married in my "going away suit", and Jack had to borrow mother's wedding ring, since mine was still at the jewelers. It all happened so fast. After the ceremony, the six of us went back to the Black Boy Restaurant for lunch (where Jack proposed), and back to our house for pictures with our movie camera. That evening Jack and I stayed at the George Hotel in central Nottingham for our wedding night.

But I was a bit disappointed. There was no bride slowly walking down the aisle in a lovely white wedding dress, with her father on her arm, no real wedding ceremony, no honeymoon, and only one night together, not knowing when we would ever see each other again. I felt so sad, cheated. I was now Mrs. Jack Hodges, "What had I done?" But little did I know my destiny would prove I had married the most wonderful man in the world. There is no one that could have loved and treasured me more than Jack. When Jack told his mother the news, she told him she was glad that I spoke English, and she turned out to be very loving and kind, even though she wanted him to marry an American girl.

The next day was May 10th, and Jack and I had to say farewell at the railroad station. It was just like a war movie playing out. Jack returned to France with his friend Utis, but not before he called a taxi to drive me home. I still had the flowers pinned to the lapel of my suit. In the taxi, the driver turned around and said, "You look like a blooming bride." I said with tears rolling down my face, "I AM a blooming bride". It certainly wasn't funny then, but as I look back now, I can laugh to myself about that specific moment. The radio in the cab was playing "One Night of Love" as it slowly pulled away from the train station, in route to my family's home.

Married and Still Entertaining

Over the next few months I continued on stage and on various radio shows with father. We even began to broadcast to the States, from York England to York Pennsylvania. Jack courted me through his regular letters, not forgetting one single day, I am sure. His letters let me know I was his wife and how much he loved me, and could not wait to for me to get to America. He was so proud to have an English wife and was on cloud nine, and so looking forward to our future. Little did either of us know what lay ahead before I could even go to America, to begin to live happily ever after with Jack. But

I have to admit, it was truly through Jack's letters that I fell in love with him.

Being married and still on stage was not what I had expected, so starting the process to actually travel and live in America was my priority. There was so much red tape, so many papers to fill out, and I had to make several trips to the American Embassy in London. Fortunately, I had a dear friend accompany me, and I truly needed her support, as it would have been so incredibly hard to do alone.

By this time Jack was flying troops back home, along with awful prisoners of war from dreadful war camps. He said he would never forget many of the shocking and gruesome sights, and concluded by telling me it was one of the worst things he had experienced during the war. After he returned home, he would not talk much about it – and I silently understood.

While Jack took supplies to Patton's Army, I kept busy on stage with father. This time we were being paid for private entertainment shows, as well as regular troop shows. The money was good, that's for sure. I was the only war bride to tell her husband *not* to send any money. I managed to stay faithful; although one fellow in the show was tempting, and I did go out with him for a drink. He had a nice car. We talked a lot and he was good company. He understood what I was going through, and it was just nice to get out for a change. My two sister's Kathleen and Joyce had already left home to be with their husbands, who were now out of the service. Gone were the days when we all would be sitting by the fire together as a family, having a good laugh. Now that was all part of the past.

On the 17th of May 1945, a professional photographer arrived at my parents' home. We had all had gotten dressed in our wedding clothes, as my dress was finally finished and so were the bridesmaids. It was simply beautiful as we all posed in the garden. Actually, it is so comical now that I recall it. The photographer left an empty place by my side for Jack, and inserted a photo

Miriam in her wedding gown with her father.

of him in his uniform. Yes, Jack was not there - just a photo. In some ways it made me feel duped once more, because it looked like he had dropped in from outer space. Regardless, it was a very special and memorable moment, during a very early time in my life that was full of mayhem and love.

Mother was a saint during the war years when we all lived together at home. There was my father, mother, three daughters and a baby boy that had to be fed on very small rations. We had lots of starches, baked beans on toast, powdered eggs and spam, all presented in various ways. We used a large toasting fork to toast the bread over the fire, and there was nothing that tasted better! After toasting, we always tried to find anything we could to put on top of it. It was so cozy, especially when we added our yummy tea to the mix of it all, which we knew how to make exceptionally well. But unfortunately, our coffee left a lot to be desired. I am pretty sure I even ate horsemeat at one point or another when we went out to dinner, which was rare. But it didn't matter, it was all food. Just a simple can of peaches was a luxury, and we would often dream of that wonderful taste.

Sweets were one of our biggest vulnerabilities, which we would all scoff up as soon as they came our way. Oh yes, the delicious Canadian huge chocolates were the ultimate best, and melted in my mouth. I suppose I need to thank my boyfriends who would bring us the chocolates, which they received from their kind girlfriends back home. Little did they know those chocolates would be eaten by another very grateful family. Considering all the hardships and fear the Green family experienced, we were all very happy together. Poor father with four females and a small baby boy, named John. Father was such a "man's man", but still showed his loving side. He bought a puppet set for little John, and it was amazing how much John could make us laugh, putting on his own shows while he was so young. I have to admit we all loved spoiling him as he was growing up.

Meanwhile, I continued to live for Jack's letters and they at least made me feel married. Finally, Jack was discharged from the Air Force, and now more than ever he wanted his wife to be with him. In 1946 Jack managed to find a nice apartment to rent in Arlington Virginia, which was not easy with all the men returning home from the war. He had furnished it with such good taste, and it even had a fireplace. The rent was fifty dollars a month, imagine that. I couldn't wait to see it.

Chapter 5
Making My Way to Jack

Salisbury Processing Camp

The official procedures to be with Jack continued to be more than startling; it was now ten months since my papers were submitted, all in order. I was preparing to leave for Tidworth England, and a processing camp in Salisbury. It had not been simple and would have been much easier to marry an Englishman, but it was too late. I will never forget the sight of mother and father, as they were clinging to each other when the day came for me to leave. We were all crying, and it was such a sad and dramatic departure. How they must have felt seeing their daughter move hundreds of miles away. When would they see her again? Would she be brave enough to face what was ahead alone? I felt so bad for how they were feeling.

I boarded the bus along with several other girls from the nearby area. When we arrived at the transition camp, they immediately took away our ration books, clothing coupons and identification cards. It felt like I was giving up my connection to England. They even charged two pounds head tax before we could even leave the country. The trunks and large suitcases went in one direction, and the rest of us went in another, with only one small case left in each of our hands.

A group of cheery Red Cross personnel greeted us, and brought us into a reception room. They handed each of us a large envelope with our names on it that included instructions on what we had to do. But oddly, my envelope did not have Mrs. Hodges on it; it had Lt. Miriam Hodges and we were all now G.I.'s. They escorted me and two other girls, Iris Hobbick and Beryl Hodge into a room that had three small army cots. We were all shocked about our living quarters. But after the first day, the three of us started talking and consulting each other on what was going on. We became wonderful friends at the camp, and later continued that friendship on the ship over to America. They called us the three musketeers and we went everywhere together.

    We spent six days at Salisbury camp, and they kept us all very busy. In the mess hall we were given trays by German prisoners of war, who were surprisingly polite to us. And it was at the mess hall where we were first introduced to American food. First, we were served fried chicken, which we had never heard of. But the amount of food was a luxury, after all the small rations we had been accustomed to. The American pancakes were different too. The English version was a very thin crepe topped with sugar and orange juice, and only served once a year on International Pancake Day. And then; oh my, I tasted my first hot dog which was absolutely delicious!

    Every day, except the first day we arrived and the last day when we left the camp, we were required to attend lectures to learn about the United States. It included where each State was located, the names of each one, and some of the local sayings and customs. I was fast at learning the currency, which at times was difficult because I was so used to pounds, shillings and pence, which is not the same now.

    On the fourth day at the camp, something very different took place, and it would be one thing I would never forget. We were asked to report to one of the larger rooms which was set up as a clinic, and were told we were going to have a physical examination. One by one, the Red Cross ladies put each of us in a small cubical surrounded by flimsy curtains. They told us to undress completely, and come out of the cubical with a small sheet wrapped around us. Reluctantly, all three of us, Iris, Beryl and I came out with our panties on. The nurses looked at us and said, "Sorry, but everything must come off". The sheets were barely long enough to cover ourselves, and we kept pulling on them to cover whatever we could. The room was cold and finally they placed all of us in a straight line facing outward. We felt like we were on display; very embarrassing. Then, all of a sudden, in marched the doctors; all male. As we stood there shaking, one man who lead the group said, "Drop your sheets and leave them off until we are through examining you." We were so horrified, no one told us about this humiliating ordeal. It seemed like ages had passed as we waited in line. Each doctor took their turn in looking us over, checking every single part of our body and even shining a light between our legs. Only after each doctor examined us thoroughly, were we able to go back and get dressed. The experience left many scars for us, and still haunts myself and my friends. After getting dressed we were told to line up in another part of the room for more shots, heaven knows what for. We were still devastated from what had just happened. After all, none of us had to ever undress in front of a group of men. It just was not done. Even though we were all GI's, we had lost our dignity, and through the next couple of days quite a number of girls decided they could not take it anymore. Some had dysentery or got so homesick that they packed what little they had and went back home. But our special group of the three musketeers decided to stick it out, although one week at that camp was more than enough for me.

The last night at the camp, we all conferred about the war years, reminiscing about all the bravery we witnessed. Finally, the last day came. The officials wished us all well, allowing us each to make one final phone call at a payphone outside the camp in Tidworth, about three hours from Nottingham.

Miriam Sails to America on the Queen Mary

Hooray! Our time had finally come to leave the camp and board the ship that would take us to America. The three of us lay on our cots the night before, wondering what the ocean voyage would be like. We had survived so far, and we were told our first sailing abroad would be on the beautiful ocean liner, the Queen Mary. Finally, after all those months of red tape and hardships, it would only be five or six more days before most of the women would see their husbands.

Early the next morning, the 23$^{rd.}$ of February, a bus arrived to take us to Southampton to board the great ship. We slowly made our way off the bus into a large building next to where the ship was docked, and asked us to stand in alphabetical order. After boarding, another group of Red Cross volunteers greeted us, and showed us to our cabins. There were 2,400 G.I. brides from all over the country, mainly the southern part of England, so it took about twenty four hours to board. But we soon learned the Queen Mary was no luxury liner. The quarters were tight and to our dismay there were no beds, just hammocks and rock hard pillows made of straw. We decided we had to make the best of it, just like all the GI's had to do.

The next day we set sail early for America. Everyone crowded to the top deck to bid farewell to our beloved England, and to toast the start of our new lives in our adopted country. Before lunch we assembled in the lounge, and the captain gave a short speech to welcome us on board. He hoped our journey across the Atlantic would be pleasant and smooth, but it turned out to be far from that.

The meals were good; different from the camp. Waiters served our meals at our table and no more standing in line. We musketeers always went to the mess hall to eat our meals together. Eating became less interesting as we sailed further across the Atlantic. The ocean waters were rough and many became seasick, but the ship continued on its course. We walked to the promenade deck to get some air and sun, which was impossible as the deck was enclosed. So we sat in deck chairs wrapped up in our heavy winter coats to get some fresh air. Later that day, I was the first of the three girls to come down with sea sickness, and then too ill to leave the cabin. The seas were getting worse and all I ate was an apple, soda crackers and seven-up. And at that very moment, all I could say to myself was, "I wish I had never met an American, I could just die." Beryl joined me soon afterwards, but Iris was the tough one. Then all three of us were quite ill together. After several days, the seas became much calmer, thank heaven, as we neared the United States. We had made our docking preparations the day before, and now were all prepped and ready for our future to unfold.

Meeting Jack in New York Harbor

It was the first day of March when we entered the New York Harbor. The captain announced we were approaching the Statue of Liberty and boy was I ever glad to see her and city of New York! It took several hours to dock, even with numerous tug boats pulling us in, but it was a joyous occasion. You could see family and friends standing on the large dock on shore, waving and cheering as they looked for their loved ones. Jack had come to New York by car with his younger brother Albert. As soon as the ship docked, he sent Albert home by train. I wondered if I would recognize Jack since it had been so long. Good thing he wore his uniform. Jack was so excited and had lived for this moment, just as I did. We were soon in each other's arms and no one else around us existed.

But it was not happy times for all. I felt so sorry for my dear friend Iris. Her husband did not come to meet her, and she had to travel all the way to Kansas on her own; how awful that would be. I had heard of husbands that left their wives stranded, even with babies. Boy, was

I lucky to not have been in that situation.

After claiming our luggage, Jack and I set off for the Aster Hotel in New York, where we were staying for two days. I could not believe everything around me, especially the food in the shop windows. Jack took me shopping and bought me a pair of platform shoes, and at the same time I bought a pair for Joyce. People were so kind; they even gave me nylons, a very rare item back then.

Jack was so loving and thrilled to have his English wife home with him at last. After fun and sightseeing in New York, we drove to Arlington Virginia. I was shocked when we reached the apartment Jack had arranged for us, after living in a house all of my life. This was different and Jack had furnished it with such taste, poor darling.

Miriam sails to America on the Queen Mary.

Chapter 6
Life with Jack in America

I tried to get comfortable with my new environment, but it was difficult and I told Jack I wanted to go back to England. He asked if we could wait until tomorrow. Sadly, I was already very homesick, but glad I waited. The big surprise was seeing Jack out of uniform, and in civilian clothes. I thought to myself, "The glamour was gone, and I was now his poor wife". But that soon passed. I did not know how to cook and Jack was a big help in teaching me. Things were different in America. I even cooked a chicken with the bag in it –ha! We laughed a lot and I was very lucky Jack was not fussy about his food. As for me, any food was a luxury. I was 100 lbs. when I arrived in America, but soon gained a little weight, because I had to try everything. It was wonderful to have so many choices. I loved ice cream, sodas and milkshakes and was on cloud nine.

Jack was now out of the air force and pilots were a dime a dozen. He could have gotten a job with the airlines, but that may have sent him overseas. He could not leave me alone in a strange country, because he knew how much I needed him and he was right. Before long Jack took a job as a salesman for a construction company, but he was not happy taking direction from someone else. Jack was not meant to be an employee - he had to be the boss.

Men who served the country were given a GI loan of six hundred dollars when they left the service, so Jack used his portion to start his own construction company. First, we bought an insulation truck because people wanted to insulate their homes to save energy. Then, we gradually expanded the business to build home additions, including kitchens, porch enclosures, adding windows, doors and so on. It was very hard at first, because we had to ring doorbells to get established in the area. Also, during that time we had very little income coming in, making it even harder to get workers to work for us until we became known. Finally, Jack got a lucky break. A friend put him in touch with construction job opportunities at the Embassy in Washington. After that, word began to spread that Jack had completed some jobs at the White House and at the vice-presidents house - Rockefeller at the time (he told me about the mirrored ceilings in the bedroom and bathroom-hard to believe). Thankfully, Jack finally began to make a decent living.

Working in America

I like to stay busy, so I took a job as a salesgirl

Painting of Miriam Hodges.

in a little dress shop in walking distance to where we lived in Virginia. The boss and his wife were Jewish and had no children. But over time they started treating me as if I was their daughter, which caused trouble in our family. They told lies to Jack about me, and tried to take me away from him. He was livid and told them off in no uncertain terms, and that was the end of that job.

My next job was on Connecticut Avenue at a very upscale posh dress shop. It was owned by a New York firm, close to the Mayflower Hotel in Washington. I assisted many movie stars and celebrities, Margaret Truman and even Jackie Kennedy, with her little sleeveless dresses. They had to have an appointment to come into the shop, as the prices were very high, so they kept the front door locked. I had landed the job through an ad in the paper, which stated they were looking for a woman who spoke foreign languages. I figured I did (in so many uncertain terms), and once again bluffed my way through, but of course with my own exclusive style and accent. Later, I was offered the manager's job with good pay, but that was too much stress, not to mention I had to be on my feet all day and then ride the bus home.

Jack and I had moved from the apartment, and bought a house with a garden. Can you believe the cost of our home was only $11,400? Jack remodeled it over time and it turned out to be fabulous.

Oh, one other very important thing I should have never waited so long to mention. Shortly after I arrived in America, Jack bless him, arranged for us to have a regular church wedding, because he knew I felt so bad that we never were able to carry out our original plans. It was at Ft. Myers Chapel in Virginia - so bitter sweet. I had brought my dress with me and a cousin of Jack's was my bridesmaid. Jack wore his uniform and was handsome as ever. The photographer had the real bride and groom in the picture this time. Jack's family was curious to see his bride and we had a beautiful reception - I only wish my family had been there.

Happy Jack.

Mother and Father's First Trip to America

In 1947 my mother and father came to America for the very first time. They wanted to see their daughter and her new home in America. It was impossible to get passage on a ship, as they were fully booked. Father told the ship reservationist they could be ready in twenty four hours, should a cancellation come through. And so it did, and they were listed as two Chinese passengers. It didn't matter to them, as long as they were on their way. But my poor fathers' health was failing, as a result of the wartime food. So their voyage ended up to be a blessing in disguise, because they raved about the food including the delicious rolls and butter served on board.

    Jack and I drove to New York to meet them, and we all stayed at a nice hotel. They were so thrilled with New York and we even saw the play "Annie Get Your Gun" on Broadway, with the original cast, including actress Ethel Merman. Father loved it, just his cup of tea, mine as well. New York at night is such a thrill with all the lights and action, especially after blackout England for all those years. They totally enjoyed the food, and eating out was a real treat, especially the seafood. Father was not sure about soft shell crab, and said he would just as soon eat a spider, but loved the large shrimp.

Jack's father and mother also got along well with my parents, and loved speaking to mother with her perfect British accent, just like mine. Mother was not shy, and Jack's parents even asked her to speak at a church in Washington, which she did so very well. We spoiled mother and father during their stay in New York with us, and it became very hard for them to return to England, because they really fell in love with America.

Once back to England, mother told her friends about their trip and the funeral homes she had seen in America. Funeral homes were something England badly needed, so believe it or not, she started one in Nottingham. England was still in bad shape from the war and had a food shortage, among other things. People were struggling to get back to a normal life, if that was possible. I'm afraid their visit made them discontent with England, as they bragged so much about America people once they got back home. Their friends didn't appreciate it and started to not like mother's comments and said, "Why did you come back?" Mother felt badly, but there was something very good that came from their trip to America. The food father ate during his trip helped him become healthier and stronger, which we were all very grateful.

Back to England in 1948

Jack and I went back to England in 1948 and flew Pan American Airlines. It was my first airline flight, and I remember it was very expensive and long. We had to leave from N.Y. and stopped in Newfoundland, then we flew to Shannon and on to Heathrow, London. They gave us box meals, which did not taste good. I was a little afraid, but it was great having my pilot husband beside me. Oh, to be in England again, it was wonderful. I knew right then how homesick I really was. It was so good to see my family and friends, and for whatever reason things seemed small to me. While in London we rented a car, and were interviewed by the local newspaper.

Jack had joined the Rotary Club back home in Virginia, and was also happy to visit several Rotary friends on our trip abroad. Everyone treated him so well. Later Jack became President of the Rotary Club in Virginia, which opened many new doors and created lasting friendships.

Going back to England helped me settle my heart better, and I was happier once I returned to the United States. I was now becoming more American, but would always love my England and continue to be very proud to be English. I felt if I were to live in America with an American husband, I should become an American citizen. So, I attended school to learn more about American history, including the political details of the Congress, Senate and many other fragments that made the world go round. I had to wait months before I knew I passed the course, which gave us another reason to celebrate life.

Chapter 7
Entertaining in Our New Home

Jacks' business was now doing much better, and we finally were able to buy a larger home located in the small town of Sleepy Hollow in Falls Church, Virginia. We were so thrilled with our new home and Jack made sure it was a showplace. It had a huge fireplace with high ceilings made of pecky cypress, and a stained glass door that you could see through from the outside. Jack had turned the garage into a quasi-English pub, so he added a carport on the side of the house.

Because it was so hot and humid, we also decided to install a swimming pool and were one of the few families to have one. It was my dream. But the process of excavating the land created mounds of dirt in front of our picture window, which went on for weeks, because the contractors had several other jobs. It was frustrating, but finally it was finished and Jack and I were like kids when we took our first swim. Our new home provided so much pleasure and we were very happy together.

Over time Jack converted the living room into the dining room, and added a large step down family room with a lounge and several sky domes, so very elegant. Then he added an additional room off the pool we called our "Pool House", complete with a sauna, bar and built in music. Jack had so many ideas and our home

Jack and Miriam laughing and
playing by the pool.

became the perfect party place for entertaining. Together, Jack and I especially enjoyed entertaining other people. We had numerous theme parties where guests would dress up in costumes. One was a roaring twenties party where we had a sign at the bottom of the driveway saying, "The Mafia Meets Here Tonight". The men came with their violin cases, dark suits and hats. The women were beautiful with their fringe dresses, even a couple showed up in old fashioned bathing suits. Jack had such an imagination. We had another successful theme party for "Famous Lovers". Jack dressed up as Onassis and I was Jackie, complete with a black wig. Then two couples arrived dressed as Adam and Eve. People just love to dress up, don't they? There was one man dressed as a woman, had a full length fur coat, polished nails and all, and he was the president of a local airlines (I won't tell). Our Rotary Club parties where just as fun! Several of the most endowed men dressed in women's bathing suits and showed up at one of our parties... Jack of course got into the act, dressed up and later ended up in the pool.

The next day we found a straw hat and a cigar floating in the pool and had a good laugh.

On another occasion, Jack and I went to a party and I had a few drinks and invited some friends back to our house for a swim. I did not mean for them to come at three in the morning, as we were exhausted and had already gone to bed. But then the doorbell rang, and several couples from the party wanted to go for a swim. I told them where to change their clothes, but there was no use. They were soon in the nude and swimming and laughing in the pool, having a ball. Poor Jack was so upset and very mad at me for what I had created. I never expected this kind of rowdy crowd, and so very late. Sure enough, the neighbors called the police. Fortunately they were so nice and just asked us to be quieter. Jack made sure everyone left in a hurry. From that point on, I decided my drinking days were over and the couple next door did not speak to us for two years; oh well, no great loss.

Too Coincidental - Friends for a Lifetime

Now, let's go back now to Margery and Bob Lloyd Davies. When I first came to America, Margery saw my name in the paper. She was a school teacher from Nottingham, and we even found out she taught Irene. She was married to Bob, who was the labor attaché at the British Embassy. We all became good friends and I baby sat their little boy Peter, who was four years old and well behaved. Their daughter was also named Virginia, and I became her Godmother. When Virginia Davies was nineteen, she lived in London and both her and her mother Margery made a trip to see me in the States. What a surprise when she arrived for a short stay and then just left Virginia with us....I always wondered why, until later.

It was summertime in Sleepy Hollow and that meant it was "pool time". Virginia would comfortably lay topless by the pool. We had a large picture window in the kitchen that looked right over the pool area. I remember Jack passed by and could not believe his eyes, as Virginia was very well endowed. She was very sexy, and it was hard to keep the men away. After a while we told her she would have to find a job.

Virginia spoke several languages and was well educated, so we thought the United Nations would be a good place for her to find a job. So off she went to New York, and she came to see us when she could on weekends. After a while she became burnt out with New York, and ended up in a commune in Scotland, probably peeling potatoes. Then one day an American cycled in, and when he met Virginia, he did not cycle out. Dennis and Virginia married and our Goddaughter Virginia became a famous painter, with a focus on Chinese brush work. She even had a showing and teaching on a public broadcasting network, such a talent. We are glad she is happy and they now both live in Virginia. Her mother Margery died soon after Virginia was left with us, fate took a hand and now I understood why she left her with us.

Bob married again, and now had a condo in Arizona. It was amazing to be in his spa and look out to see snowcapped mountains. Arizona is a lovely part of the country. We liked his new wife Grace, as they seemed to be well suited for each other.

Bob and Grace visited us when we lived in Sleepy Hollow, and also in Florida where we took them shopping on Worth Avenue in Palm Beach. We had to laugh when we went into a very upscale thrift store and suddenly heard lovely classical music. We looked around and there was Bob playing a baby grand piano someone had donated. So many people gathered around, as he gave quite a performance. I bet that was a first.

Bob was very British, and Margery and he used to have a lovely home in northwest England in a very prestigious area called "Harrow on the Hill". Back in the early years, Jack and I visited them and we all went on holiday together. They were very good people.

Jean was also another friend of mine who

worked at the British Embassy. Her husband Bernie was so talented and played the accordion, which was very popular at our parties. They came to one of our fancy costume parties dressed as the "Cockney Pearls King and Queen". Their outfits were made of all pearls, even their hats. What a fun couple.

It was a miserable ending for Jean. We did not know why, but she took her own life, so sad. We had so many friends with many different personalities, from different walks of life and different places around the globe. All of them were very interesting; and we just lucky to have known them all.

After Five - Fun & Fabulous Festivities

Back in those days, Jack and I enjoyed a cocktail or two. One of our favorite drinks were Gin and Tonic or Scotch and Soda. We found having a cocktail was a wonderful way to relax. Martini's and Whiskey Sours were also popular, and of course, a special liquor after a big dinner party. During the holidays, a creamy Brandy Alexander was the drink of choice, and Jack loved a good wine or champagne. But Jack was not much of a drinker, and I was lucky for that.

Jack and I have had few funny drinking experiences, and have ended up crashing our share of parties over the years. I laugh now when I remember those days. One time we crashed a wedding reception in Canada, which was really a mistake. We thought we were in a convention room, until we saw all the gifts on a large table. But it was too difficult to escape, so we stayed and had a great time.

Another time in Vero Beach, we had just been to a party that ended too early for us, and since we were all dressed up, we hated to go home. When driving home we noticed a lot of lights on at a small commercial shop, located in what is called "The Village Shops". So we stopped the car and joined the affair. Right after we entered, a glass of champagne was placed in our hands and food was being passed around. We recognized a friend and he came up to us and said "You were invited for tomorrow night". We laughed and said, "How could we make such a mistake?" Of course we did not return the next evening.

Another time in Bermuda, Jack wanted to play golf and made a new friend with a doctor from San Francisco, who also wanted to play. We had taken our mopeds to the golf course, which was connected with a very nice hotel and pool. I decided to wait for Jack by the hotel pool, and arranged to meet him later on. A nice man directed me to a lounge chair, complete with cushions, towels etc., in a lovely setting with very few people around. At four o'clock in the afternoon I was served a delicious tea, but did not tell the waiter I was not a guest of the hotel. I suppose when this man saw Jack going to play golf, he just assumed we were staying there. Another bluff! But Jack's new golf partner invited us for dinner that night, and once more we had a picture perfect day. His wife was very charming, and later we got back on our mopeds and rode off into the sunset. Such fun living life in the moment! Life has been so interesting. Around every corner there was always something enjoyable to do and laughs to be had.

While in Bermuda we also hired a sailboat with a captain, who was quite old. He was so interesting and took us into his cabin below, and showed us lots of pictures of movie stars and celebrities. But I have to admit, all of that drinking and partying is a thing of the past now. I decided I did not need the hard stuff to have a good time, so now wine fits right in.

Chapter 8
Sylvia, Mark and Meaningful Memories

I took another sales position at another ladies-wear store. I became their bridal consultant and then moved on to sell furs. I never was very good at selling the smaller items, so this kept me interested and busy for a short while. Later I took on office work, but was a disaster on the switchboard. My boss at the ladies store was from Boston and seemed hard to get to know, but we both liked each other. He even entrusted me to do some buying for his store on one of my trips to London.

Along with my job, I added enjoyable activities such as performing at the local Women's Club charity show. I presented a "Gypsy Act", and did a performance to the song "Let Me Entertain You". The song implied I would be dancing, and slowly taking my clothes off. I had on a large men's camel coat and pretended I had nothing on underneath. But, I did have on a skimpy bathing suit and fooled everyone again. It was so much fun making my entrance to introduce each act - which reminded me of being an entertainer once again. It was so enjoyable!

Pool Time Activities

It was at this particular women's store I made many good friends, and one very special one named Sylvia Declue, from Austria. We have been like sisters

Sylvia and Miriam relaxing in the swimming pool in Virginia.

ever since. Sylvia was married to a good looking American named Norman, who had been in the Navy during the war. The four of us began to spend every weekend together. Jack would make his favorite Pink Daiquiris' and serve them by the pool. It was a shame when we would have to dive in and sober up. When at Sylvia's and Norman's, she would cook a great dinner (she was such a fantastic cook), and afterwards we would watch a movie or just chat away. They were wonderful friends to us.

    One afternoon Sylvia and I were sun bathing naked by our pool. Our home was very, very private and only someone in the air could have seen us. Then the doorbell rang and I grabbed a towel and quickly wrapped it around me. I answered the door, and there stood a man who introduced himself as a preacher from England. Jack had met him before at the Rotary Club, and had encouraged him to come and meet his English wife. Sylvia and I asked him in, but he then continued to stay a long time, and we still only had our towels on. When he left, he gave us both a hug. In the back of my mind I was thinking, "I hope my towel stays on". After he left we both had a good giggle. I remember when I told Jack the story he said, "That was bad timing", and I agreed. But that didn't stop me from going back to getting sun all over my body, to the point of burning my derriere. Sylvia said, "Oh don't worry, sour cream will take the sting out". My sunburn was bright red and very painful. Jack and Norman had joined us after work that same day and announced they had a treat for us. They were taking us to dinner at a very special restaurant called "Peter Pan", wow! We did not dare to mention my sunburn, because it was a very long drive to the restaurant, OUCH…but I survived.

Sylvia was very beautiful and had so much class, and went to a lot of our parties. She became very tired of being on her feet all day at the dress shop, so Jack gave her a job at his office. Jack also sponsored Sylvia's brother Helmuth, who was living in Australia. This enabled him, his wife and children the opportunity to come to America with a job waiting for him at Jack's company as a salesman. However, after a very short time here, Helmuth decided to leave our company. Jack had spent a lot of time training him, but Helmuth wanted to open his own contracting business with a friend who did asbestos work. We think that was what killed him at an early age.

Helmuth left his wife and children for a German

Miriam sunbathing.

married woman. He did this after his wife helped him during the very hardest of times abroad. Really, she did not deserve to be treated so badly. Too bad he did not just have an affair. It was so hard for the children, and Sylvia disowned him, but somehow we got them back together. They were family to us and Helmuth should have never left the "Hodges Company" on his way up the ladder. Helmuth helped build our pool house and had some very good ideas.

Sylvia went to Austria for a visit, but before she left the country, the four of us drove to New York and had lunch at the famous "Lindy's", known for its cheesecake. Sylvia and I shared everything, but Sylvia told the waiter "We do not share our coffee". For some reason the waiter broke up laughing, so he gave her a Lindy ashtray as a gift. We really have had some good laughs. Sylvia was gone a very long time in Austria, and

Mark and little Virginia by the pool in Sleepy Hollow, Virginia.

Norman her husband spent a lot of time with us, as he was very lonely without her. For some reason Sylvia kept extending her trip and finally she returned. I missed her so much.

The Birth of Mark

In 1964 Sylvia gave birth to a baby boy named Mark. I had Mark in my life early, as I often walked with Sylvia during her pregnancy around the Sleepy Hollow neighborhood. I made sure I gave her a shower that included all of her friends, and even a huge stork. But it was a sad day when we had to find a new home for her two poodles, as none of us felt it would be good to have with a new baby.

In later years Mark joined the naval academy close to Virginia, and Sylvia and Norman moved to Cocoa Beach Florida to a nice home near the river. Mark became part of our family and came to see us on weekends, often with his navy buddies and loads of laundry. He took over the pool house and played his own music. We gave him a lot of space and he loved it. It was exciting to see him as a young plebe with a shaved head, and then four years later graduating and throwing his hat in the air with other grads. Now he was an officer and a gentleman, and we were so proud of him. He still talks about breakfast at the Hodges that Jack would make him. Jack would prepare as many as thirteen waffles with his mother's old waffle iron, and pass them through from the kitchen window to the pool patio just for Mark.

Sylvia and Norman came to help us with the graduation party we gave for Mark in Virginia. We invited Mark's friends and lots of their friends too. Those were lively happy times. Mark was going with a girl from the academy, and someone pushed both of them into the pool and they ended up in the sauna. They became engaged, but it did not last. When Mark left, I missed his weekend visits and later he became a captain in the Navy. I couldn't believe our boy was being saluted by all the crew and officers. What a day and again; so proud!

But Mark was not so lucky in love. He was married twice. The first was a disaster, and he is now divorced with the second. They did have two dear children, and Mark finally left the Navy to be close to them in California. His ex-wife married the man she left him for, and at least for the children's sake, they have a good relationship. Mark seems happy and comes to Florida to visit. One day I hope he finds the right partner to share his life with, as he is so special and deserves the very best.

Mark landed a very good job and everyone soon found out how great of an asset he was. He was very smart and talented, and would be an advantage to any company he went to work with. As for me, well I did not get my admiral as I thought I would. Oh well, I could dream….or it was just not meant to be.

Sylvia and I have been very close friends now for over fifty years, and have shared many wonderful memories. There is a very close bond between us. Thank you Sylvia for being there for me, and for sharing Mark. Having you both in my life means so very much. Jack loved you both.

Father and Mother Return to America

Mother and father came back to visit again from England, and loved our new house. They saw it before the lovely living room and pool house were added. But they especially loved the pub room, which was very special for them. We took them to Florida and traveled through many states throughout America.

Father stayed so long in America that we had to tell him he needed to get a job. One of our friends at the British Embassy in a high position came through, and found him work in Washington. He became very popular, but it was tiring as he had to commute back and forth, which took a toll. Jack decided to give father a job with the Hodges Company. People loved his personality and accent. Jack had him working in the office and also had him canvass homes for business leads. Once my father had one foot in the door selling the services of Hodges Construction, Jack would come in after him to close the deal; what a team!

After fourteen months father became homesick; a long time to be away. So both mother and father sailed back to England by ship. At that very same time, Eleanor Roosevelt was on her way to London to unveil the Statue of Franklin. Father being the performer he was, performed one night at the ship's concert. While on board performing he met Mrs. Roosevelt, as she personally greeted the artists after the show. He said he would never forget her saying how much she enjoyed his humor, and it was such fun to have a good laugh. While the cruise back to England ended up being a rough voyage, my parents were good sailors and made it back safely.

Miriam at 30 years old on the Queen Elizabeth.

Brief encounter with James Andrew on the Queen Elizabeth.

Chapter 9
Miriam's Memorable Voyage

Meeting James Andrew

In 1955, I sailed back to England on the Queen Elizabeth. Jack was to join me later and was very sad to see the ship depart. I was thirty years old and it would be my best year ever. On the first day I decided to get some sun on deck. I found a lounge chair and fell asleep. When I woke, there was a very tall handsome man sitting next to me. He smiled and said, "Wow". We were served afternoon tea and started chatting. His name was James Andrews, a divorced American lawyer from Ohio, and was traveling with another lawyer friend on business. We met again that evening for cocktails and dinner, and ended up staying together the entire voyage. I guess after ten years of marriage, I became "smitten". We did not sleep together and I was faithful to Jack, but I have to admit I was tempted since we were so attracted to each other. We sadly parted company after the ship docked, but I did keep a special piece of memorabilia. On a farewell dinner menu, Jim autographed "I'll always envy the American who made a colonist of you. The empires loss is our gain." Another ship mate wrote "To a most charming ambassadress from England, a fine advertisement for shipboard travel". The QE will always have fond memories for me.

Jack had bought a car before we left and had it shipped first class on the ship. It was a very large nomad station wagon. He had such a hard time getting a rental car when we were in England in the past, he just decided to buy a car and ship it over. But it was Ted (Joyce's husband), that came to pick me up and bring me to Nottingham. Obviously, I had to tell Jack about my brief encounter with Jim on the ship. Jim ended up coming to see Jack and me when he had business in Washington. He stayed at the Mayfair Hotel and one evening we met him for a drink. Jack liked him and told me later that he could see the attraction. I don't know another husband who would have been so understanding. Jack was just so glad I was HIS.

1950's Travel Highlights

We traveled a lot in the 1950's, including many visits to Canada to see Irene and Lee, and the four of us visited much of Europe by car. In Germany we stopped to look at a menu that was posted outside a diner, and a man came up and asked if he could help us decide. Jack invited him to join us and it turned out he had been a German pilot. It was strange sitting with an American and a German pilot at the same time. Lee's brother was killed by a German pilot, but the war was over and one has to move on.

Another year we made a spur of the moment decision to go back to Canada to visit with Irene and Lee on New Year's Eve. They had invited us to attend a party at the officers club in Toronto, as Lee had stayed in the RCAF. I had forgotten to pack an evening dress for New Year's, which turned out to be a blessing in disguise. The gown I purchased was a beauty; super white in color and made of crepe material, with a shimmering silver top. It was the era of the mini skirt, so of course I was so with it, and I had my hair done just to top it off. I danced all night with many partners, sad to say. And there is more to this dress that was so eloquent. I also took it with me to beautiful Bermuda, where Jack and I frequently visited.

I loved to see the handsome policeman directing traffic in their Bermuda shorts and hats. Anyway, while on the island, a small thunderstorm developed and we needed to take shelter in someone's doorway. But unfortunately, I had on that same white dress that I wore on New Year's Eve in Toronto. I found out quickly that it was not a good idea to get my dress wet. The funny part is that it began to shrink, because of the material. Imagine walking through the hotel lobby all wet in that dress, so glad I had a picture taken - as it was a special memory.

Responsibilities of the Heart

In 1971 I went back to England again to see my family. I knew I had to go home as father was very ill and mother was not well either. I couldn't believe my two sisters had not taken a hand to help them, especially Kathleen. I traveled three thousand miles, and as soon as I saw mother I took her to the hospital to help solve her medical issues. Father was not eating much either and was slowly fading away. He wanted me by his side much of the time to watch a variety of TV shows, and share all the musicals he loved. I did a lot of needed improvements to the house while I was there, including new carpets etc., with no help.

One day while I was there I went into town shopping, and decided to take the local bus. I met a very nice lady and we started chatting. I told her my situation, how mother badly needed help and I needed to go back to America. There was no way I could go back to America without figuring this out. It just so happened this woman was looking for a job, and what I had described was exactly the type of work she could do. Mother was pleased and also liked her, which made leaving a bit easier. She turned out to be a godsend when father passed away.

It was time for my departure and mother gave me a note to give to Jack. It read "My dear son, I just cannot thank you enough for sending me your darling wife. She has been such an angel to us. They threw away the pattern after she was born. Cherish her, for which I know you will, as she is an angel here on earth. This is a fond good-bye from two people who can never repay you. All my best wishers for your future happiness. Love, Mother". That letter brought tears to both of our eyes. And as for my poor father, he had been a heavy smoker from an early age. And unfortunately he paid the price with his life. He of course would want me to tell you his story, and I am proud to do so.

My Father - John William Green

John William Green was known as Jonnie, a BBC comedian in all classes of entertainment. He came from a very good family, being the only son with many sisters. Starting at a very young age, John served in the trenches of World War 1 for four years, mostly in France. Sarah, his wife, was left alone with a new born baby named Kathleen. Mother never forgave the German's for those lost years. It was during this war that father discovered he had a talent for making people laugh, so he created a small show. Some of the servicemen were still wearing makeup from performing when they were sent back to fight in the trenches. John came back safe; a miracle, but an older and wiser man, like many others that survived the "war to end all wars".

There were few jobs back then, and father worked hard day and night. He cleaned a large commercial bank at night to earn extra money. I remember when he would tell a story about how he enjoyed a night out on just a shilling. He never rode a bus and must have walked miles in his lifetime. He became a French wood polisher and learned the trade, which is now a lost art.

In 1922 father joined a concert party called "The Broadcasters". He became their producer and leading comedian for several years. In the 1930's he developed a new concert party (a traveling show of songs and comedy), including a production for the opening chorus, concerted items and gags. He was so talented that he did both the singers role and a comedy spot. Microphones were rare in those days, so you had to have a good strong voice to be heard by the people in the back.

    The outbreak of World War II found Jonnie Green amongst the first to organize shows for the war troops. It was the start of what eventually became the sum total of seventeen local concert parties. Father and his team traveled in black out conditions to military camps, gun sights, hospitals, R.A.F. bases and church halls. Wherever there was a wartime audience starved for entertainment, my father (Jonnie) was there. The reward may have only been a mug of hot cocoa, but it was a job undertaken with pride and professionalism.

    Father gave joy to so many people, and was born with the talent of a natural comedian. What a gift! He even gave his time and service to charities and was wonderful with children. I still have a picture of him on the stage and every child has a smile in the audience. Giving pleasure to all those who were less fortunate, including those in hospitals, made him complete. I will always be proud of my dear father.

Chapter 10
Life Decisions and Celebrations

In 1970 Jack and I celebrated our 25th wedding anniversary, and took a wonderful trip to Hawaii. Jack loved music, so he picked right up on playing the Hawaiian guitar. And I so loved the Hawaiian food, fruit and culture. We visited several islands by sea plane and ferry, and truly felt like we were in paradise. All of the islands with their natural beauty had something different to offer, including lush flora, steep cliffs, waterfalls and volcanic rock. Not to mention the white sandy beaches surrounded by an amazing ocean. An incredible site to see! During our stay we attended a local Rotary Lunch and as always, the people were incredibly welcoming and went all out for us. We loved Hawaii and happily went back another time on business.

A New Business Opportunity
Once back in Virginia, Jack went back to work and was presented with a new business opportunity. You see, Jack rented his office space in an area that had a lot of small businesses, similar to a strip mall. The man that owned the property liked Jack and wanted to retire, so he offered Jack a deal. If Jack bought the building for eighty thousand dollars, there would be an income from the different shops or offices. So Jack did. But poor Jack could not sleep that night thinking about the deal he had

just made. Little did he know that his decision was a very smart move. Fortunately one of Jack's Rotary friends named Carrol Wright was a real estate appraiser, and very bright. Carrol told Jack the land was very valuable and would be a great site for motel. A bunch of women told Jack he could not build a motel there, because it was a historical site. But before anything could be stopped, Jack and Carrol quickly had it torn down, and a new motel was built. Building this motel was a great decision. We had a marvelous grand opening, which even came with a bag lady, who stuffed her bag with enough food for a month. We had to laugh, the motel was had a bridal suite with a mirrored ceiling. Then with an added stroke of luck, we were told the Washington area metro system would come to our doorstop, only twelve minutes to the White House.

Carrol had been a prisoner of war in solitary confinement for two years, and had it rough, leaving terrible scars. Then his wife died, so he spent a lot of time at our house. We tried to help him as much as we could, and even gave Carrols' son a job at the motel taking care of the books. But his son ended up cheating us, taking a huge amount of money. This news devastated Carrol when he found out. We sold the motel after quite a while, which had been a good investment, despite the losses. We had fun owning it and enjoyed staying there when in town, but it was time once more to move on.

After selling the motel, Jack and I decided to purchase a large motor home from Albert, who was already in the car business. We had many pleasurable times going to the shopping outlets in Pennsylvania, and then spending the night in the parking lot in our motor home. What fun! We would wake up the next morning, and after breakfast we would shop till we dropped. While traveling through the beautiful countryside in our motor home, we stumbled on a place where the book "A Small Hotel" was written, authored by Robert Olen Butler. We even bought a farm, and made a little money when we sold it to Jacks' cousin Jane. She still lives there with her family. Albert, Jack's brother, sadly went broke with his car business. So Jack took him into his business, because he thought he was a good salesman and had big ideas. But that backfired when Albert started another business on the side, which Jack did not like. Jack realized Albert and him did not think alike, as he was only out for the almighty dollar.

Our Roger
While in Virginia we received a phone call from one of our Rotary friends, who moved to Orlando, Florida. They called us to see if we would consider having their son visit us for a while in Virginia, so that he could see Washington. He was from England and his name was Roger Dobson. We had just had a house full of guests, so I was not too crazy about the idea, but agreed as long as he was able to take care of himself. So, Jack and I went to the bus station to pick him up, and when I saw him it was love at first sight. He was so handsome and only twenty one years of age, and when he smiled at me, I just melted. Roger turned out to be so special and kind, and had a personality that oozed out of him with charm. Jack and I could not do enough for him. He became our family, and after a few days away sightseeing, we could not wait for him to come back to have dinner with us. We were so sad to see Roger leave. He wanted to continue to travel, so we called friends in New York and California for him to visit them. Everyone embraced his charm and personality and were pleased to have met him.
Roger also visited us again after we had moved to the Moorings in Vero Beach Florida. Now he has a wife named Katie, and two children, a boy named Oliver and a girl Sophie. We took them all to Palm Beach, and shared the superb sandy beaches and the ever-changing colors of the Atlantic Ocean, all along the east coast of Florida. Roger's parents also came to visit and were from the Windermere Lake District in London. Like Roger, they were very special to us. Later, we stayed with them on one of our trips to Scotland, and treated us like

royalty, sharing their lovely home and gardens. We had a wonderful time, and here once again, the Rotary Club brought distinctive relationships that really mattered into our lives.

While in London we also stayed at Roger's and Kate's townhouse, or should I say, in the outskirts of London called "Hounds Gate". They were away on holiday, so we had their place to ourselves. Jack was great and we went into London to see the shows. But traveling back and forth by taxi late at night became difficult. The drivers did not want to go that far out of London, as they wanted a short fare for more money. Later, Jack found out he could park his car for free after six o'clock in the evening. This was perfect! So we would drive in into London and then back to Roger's to see the good shows. "Barnham" was one of the musicals, which played at the London Palladium, and had six hundred and fifty five performances. Obviously, I was in heaven once more with all the memories of my childhood.

Our dear Roger, he died much too young of a brain tumor. We were all heartbroken and it was so hard to believe. Poor Kate and their children, his mother and

Jack, Miriam and Roger relaxing by the pool.

father, and of course Roger himself will always be in our hearts. At least we had him for a little while......life is just not fair. Kate keeps in touch. The children are all grown and both went to college and have good jobs, including Kate. She never remarried, as Roger was a hard act to follow. His mother and father are now with him. It's true the good die young, but why?

Chapter 11
A Vacation Home & Holiday Memories

Our Condo at the Racquet Club
    In 1978 we went to Florida, and visited Sylvia and Norman and two other Virginia friends. Both couples had condominiums in Florida. We also thought it would be nice to have a place in Florida for vacations, and fell in love with Vero Beach. So, we decided to start looking around for property. We finally found what we wanted at a condo called the Racquet Club. It was on the third floor and had a lovely view of the ocean and boardwalk. Another balcony overlooked the pool and tennis courts. It was all in walking distance of the little beach town of Vero Beach, which was full of small shops, great eating places, and a few hotels and motels.
    With the help of a neighbor, we all became good tennis players and played at the tennis complex in our condo. The friends we made were so entertaining, and there was a large club house that hosted numerous parties. There was one special one where Jack dressed up in a tennis dress and wore my blonde wig and tights. Jack had great legs and no one dreamed it was him. Boy, did we have a laugh, as Jack was such a character. And there were many other times Jack and I would just enjoy ourselves around the pool or at the beach. Wow, what a life!

Jack and Miriam laughing and enjoying themselves at the Racquet Club in Vero Beach.

There were two special friends we became very fond of while living at the Racquet Club in Vero Beach. Jack and Pat Norberg were from Rancho Santa Fe, California. They also had a condo at the same place we did, and we all went out together often. Pat would take me to Palm Beach shopping, and we would have a great girl's day out. We also visited them in their lovely home in California overlooking the Polo grounds. They also had a daughter named Karen that I loved, and she eventually moved to Hawaii. She occasionally would come and visit me, and later got married. Jack Norberg loved old movies, just like me and we talked regularly about all the old movie stars. He would say, "Do you remember so and so?" and of course I always did. We loved California, especially the coast line. We were so lucky to be able to travel and see it all.

Jack and I truly loved life in Florida, and it was so good to be near Sylvia and Norman. They lived just an hour and a half away in Cocoa Beach. They belonged to the officers club at St. Patrick's Air Force Base, which was just three miles south of where they lived. We often would join them for a super champagne brunch on a Sunday; and occasionally taking other friends with us. And of course, their New Year's Eve party was always wonderful, because as you know, I just love dancing.

Remembering the Holidays as a Child

I always loved the holidays, but Christmas would always become a sad occasion for me, especially in my early married life. I so missed my family. Remembering my growing up years, father would decorate the hall with so many fairy lights, as we called them. We would all gather around the piano singing Christmas carols, while a lovely fire was burning in the fireplace. Our Christmas gifts were small and placed in a pillow case by our bed while we were asleep. We were not spoiled, as many children are now. In the war years we would invite servicemen to the house, who were very lonely and loved being with a family. Sometimes they would spend the night and we would hide their coats in little John's room. Father would come down the next morning for breakfast, and remark how nice the young men were, but he was glad they had left…."Enough was enough" he said. Then he would be surprised when they appeared that morning in the kitchen an hour later, saying "Good morning Mr. Green". Father was a sport and shared his small rations with them, and often they would bring us goodies too. I remember when Jack spent his first Christmas with us in England. Oh how I cherish those years.

Christmas Time and the "Ship of Fools"

While Jack and I lived in Virginia for the most part, we decided to have a party on Christmas Eve and invited many friends. We thought people would have their own plans and not come, but we were pleasantly surprised how much they loved the idea. It turned out to be a yearly event that all of our friends looked forward to, but it was a lot of work.

    Another Christmas we decided to escape during the holidays and took a cruise to Nassau, in the Bahamas. It was a good time to take a break from the business, so we boarded a ship in New York and dined with other couples at a large table. We always enjoyed meeting new people. We were introduced to an elderly gentleman, a gay man in his late forties and two Jewish girls about twenty five from New York, which made six of us. At first, it seemed like a strange group, but at the end of the trip we all became good friends. We thought the elderly man had been given the trip by his family, to get him out of the way. He was so nice and even held a cocktail party for us and was really good company.

    One night in Nassau we went into town and decided to go dancing at a place called "Dirty Dicks". We took the two young girls with us and also met some British sailors off a ship that was there in port. I talked to one sailor who was very young, and said he was from Nottingham. When I told him I was from there as well, he hugged me and started to cry. Talk about homesick, I felt so bad for him, so far from home.

    Then we met two middle aged ladies who were also from Virginia on our trip. We became good friends with them and met up with them on the island and had drinks with them at the bar. Turns out they were very well known in the horse country of Middleburg, Virginia and had a lovely home there. Once back home in Virginia we met them again and attended the Gold Cup Races. The Gold Cup is quite an event and showed some of the finest horses in the world. They also attended some of our pool parties and we were grateful to be able to return such hospitality to both of them. It is so nice to meet new people and share good times. I called that cruise "a ship of fools" all escaping Christmas, but we had a superb time.

Chapter 12
40 Years of Wonderful Memories

Our 40th Wedding Anniversary
     While it was our 40th wedding anniversary, life's challenges were not too far behind, and over time things became unsettling. While back in Virginia we missed our happy times in Florida, and of course I always had my heart in England. So in 1985 we went to England to celebrate our 40th wedding anniversary. There was a big sign in my home town of Nottingham that read "Vie Sweethearts Back in Town". We were on TV, our wartime story told and people would stop from all over to chat. It was so exhilarating and we loved the attention.
     While in England we took a boat ride with some friends named Wally and June. Wally was "Mr. Britton", and really built well. They both came to visit us in Florida later on, and were really taken back with our exciting lifestyle. They especially loved our pool and had one built in their own home in England upon their return. Wally and Mary were kind enough to arrange for Jack to go to his old Air Force base in Cottesmore, which was a real thrill for him. They truly were wonderful friends. We had a big reception at Grange Farms in Nottingham, and Kate and Roger even joined us.
     During our stay, we visited Gwen and Harold who owned a home overlooking the sea, in "Frinton on

Miriam and Jack's 40th wedding anniversary celebration in England.

the Sea"; a small seaside town in Essex. I was Gwen's bridesmaid many years past, and Harold was an English fighter pilot. They entertained us wonderfully and we were there to repay them when they came to stay with us. A huge car and driver picked us up at our hotel in London, and took us to the Savoy for breakfast, where they joined us. From there, we were driven to Windsor to see the races and the driver spread out a super meal on the grass by the car with champagne - the works. It was high tea time, and we ended up at the theatre, then taken back to our hotel. What a day of royalty! It must have cost them a mint, not to mention they even treated us to a home cooked meal out in the country. I had never seen so much home cooking for such a small family. Gwen and Harold knew how to treat us and how to live it up at the same time, and we truly appreciated it.

On another trip to England, we drove to the Orlando Airport (about two hours away from Vero), only to find out our plane would be a day late. A nice English couple gave us the news, so we stayed at a very pleasant local hotel compliments of BOAC. We became good friends with the Stephenson's in a short time, and they were a lot of fun. They told us to write to Sir Colin, head of BOAC, and complain about the previous delay and inconvenience when we returned to America. And we did and within a short time, we received a return letter with a voucher for four hundred dollars. That was great! So we used that voucher for our next vacation. We kept in touch with our new friends and even stayed at their home. They lived close to London and had a lovely family with two children; a boy and girl. They took us to a buffet lunch in Gatwick at a Hilton Hotel. It was expensive, but was the best meal I had ever had on any of our travels. Don't tell me England does not have good food, and the presentation was outstanding. We still exchange Christmas greetings. So interesting how fate often seems to be coincidental, and how it all can become very meaningful in one's life.

After both my father and Jacks' father died, both of our mothers came to stay with us and were good company. Mother was treated royally by our friends. One time when we went to Hawaii for business, she stayed with our good friend Betty whose husband was a Judge. Betty loved having mother stay with her and mother loved being with them. Believe it or not, they were not pleased to see us return. You see, my mother was good company wherever she went and everyone loved her. But it was time for mother to return home to England, as father needed her. Mother was eighty now and in a wheelchair, so she flew home vs. taking passage. She had so many beautiful sayings and taught me so much. There were many things I thought of I wanted to ask her after it was too late, but I know she still watches over me. Two months later after she returned to England, she died. She just laid on the sofa with her hands crossed and went to sleep. Her mind was great till the end, but her body could not keep up.

The "JOY" of My Sister Joyce

After mother passed, my sister Joyce and her husband Ted came for a visit. Joyce was the second daughter and born in 1920. She was true to her name, a real joy to be around. At the age of eleven she met Edward Smith, kindly known as Ted. His family lived on the same street as ours and they became friends. Mother would let Joyce go out with Ted once she became a bit older, but only as long as they took me along. They tried many ways to get rid of me so they could be alone, even took me to see the worst horror films ever, but it didn't work because I loved scary movies! Joyce and Ted became sweethearts early in the war and Ted joined the Navy. They got married when he managed to get leave, and I was her bridesmaid.

Joyce lived at home and worked at the food office along with becoming an air raid spotter during World War II. When the sirens went off, she became so scared that she spent most of her time in the bathroom. Once the war was over, Ted left the Navy and returned home to work for his father. That was a big mistake. Ted had a talent for designing and making formal dresses, especially evening attire. He made them for Joyce, as their hobby was ballroom dancing, and they won many competitions. He also made dresses for me to wear on stage, which was the envy of all my friends. What a shame he did not pursue his God given talent, but money was very scarce.

Joyce and Ted lived over his father's shop on a street that had other stores. In 1947 their daughter Mary was born. She was a very sweet child that I have been very fond of, just like a daughter. After many hard working years in the fine china business, they managed to buy a lovely home in the country in a small suburb of Nottingham called "Toton". They worked the local markets and knew how to sell their products to make a profit. Over time they developed a profitable wholesale china business, including a large warehouse which sold to retail shops. Unfortunately, small boutique china shops are now a thing of the past. Now department stores have taken over, putting many people out of business. No one buys much china anymore, but at least the younger generations seem happy drinking from an "ugly mug", as they call it. I remember mother always wanted to have her cup of tea in a china cup, and I wouldn't have it any other way. I was very close to Ted and Joyce. After all, Ted had been in my life since I was six years old. It was wonderful that Ted and Joyce were able to visit Jack and me later in life, in Vero Beach. But both of them had health problems, and were so very brave and positive - always looking at the brighter side of life. Ted, like father, was a heavy smoker and it took its toll and ended his life. Joyce could not face life without Ted and became very ill and passed away from cancer.

During this time, their daughter Mary was married to Adrian, and they had a little girl named Virginia. They took over Ted and Joyce's china business. Ted had also inherited some land from his father by the river, where there were several small holiday cottages in bad repair. When Ted departed us, Mary and Adrian worked hard to renovate the cottages and placed them up for rent. They had no problem finding renters, as it was a lovely location. They also kept one for themselves. Irene and I had a holiday at one of the cottages one time when her father rented one. We were very little girls then, and were sad to see Mary sell their home in Toton...guess too many memories. I was fortunate for the little time I had Joyce and Ted in my life. We had so many happy times together. They taught me how to laugh and deal with the "not so good times", balancing both the good with the bad, and that takes experience, patience and hope.

My Sister Kathleen

My sister Kathleen was the eldest daughter and eleven years older than me. Born in 1914, she soon would be left alone with just mother, because father was fighting in World War I. Beautiful and talented, Kathleen learned to play the piano just by humming a tune, but Joyce and

I were hopeless and needed a private tutor. She married Jim and they had a lovely home in the country. This was very difficult for her, and she was unhappy because she was raised in the city and the country life just became dull. In 1940 Jim joined the RAF (Royal Air Force), so Kathleen came home to live and went on to join fathers' entertainment show. Jim never left England and would come back to our house when he was on leave.

    In 1942, Kathleen had a son named John and he became very special to us. John was so handsome and a charmer. My boyfriends loved to take him out and we all spoiled him rotten. On certain occasions, my family would go out for the evening and I was left to babysit John and put him to bed. Then, I quietly would go downstairs and meet my boyfriend. Just when I thought he was asleep, I would hear a little voice from the top of the staircase balcony calling "Auntie Meum? Are you there?" he was too young to say Miriam - so cute. During those certain moments I thought to myself, with all kidding aside, maybe he isn't so adorable, ha-ha.

    In 1946, just after Jim left the service, Kathleen took a job for the town clerk and gave birth to a lovely daughter named Marilyn. Kathleen was able to put both her children, John and Lynn (as we call Marilyn now) through college playing the piano and was also able to get some grants to help out. It is a shame Kathleen was never able to visit me in America. She would have loved it as she was so outgoing. Later in life, Lynn married Barry and they both came to Florida several times to stay with us. They loved America, and on one visit they brought their son Tom, whom we dearly loved. Jack and I were able to visit Lynn and her husband in Cotswold, where they had a nice little home. We were fortunate on one particular occasion when one of Lynn's neighbors was away on a trip, and she worked it out so that we could stay at their home.

    Then, without notice, my sister Kathleen lost Jim suddenly. He had left for work one day and found out through a knock on her door that Jim had died. Such a shock for all! At the end of her days, Lynn found a nice apartment near their home, and was happy and content.

    I feel so pleased to have been called a "mistake", or so I was told by my parents. I am grateful for my wonderful parents and my two sisters. There are so many other things I would have loved to have known about their lives. They were both so fun loving and helped to make my earlier life complete and whole. I continue to be saddened that both of them died of cancer, a horrible disease.

Chapter 13
The 70's and 80's

Grooving in the 70's

Memories, memories and more memories. As you can tell, Jack and I loved entertaining, going to parties and having visitors full of family and friends. Having fun and sharing those moments with you has been great therapy. We loved hosting costume parties and some were funnier than others. One costume party that Jack and I were invited to was at the British Embassy. I dressed up as a prostitute; you know…..the London kind. In London, you could always spot them a mile away, mainly because they wore tacky outfits; how fitting...ha! Anyway, Jack had his army shirt and pants on, and even wore a helmet. He said, "I am going as what I am supposed to be". I said, "What does it matter as long as we have fun", and he agreed. Once at the Embassy entrance, a nicely dressed woman saw Jack and said, "Good evening General Patton". Wow, he sure looked the part! We won a bottle of good scotch and had a laugh. Once more, a lot of bluffs that were loads of fun and full of laughs.

When Mary and Adrian (Ted and Joyce's daughter and son-in-law) came for a visit to Virginia, and we took them to Pennsylvania. They saw the Amish people and their little buggies, which they were amazed with. We also took them on a trip to Florida in our big motor home. When their daughter Virginia was eighteen months old, they came back to see us. Funny thing, Virginia seemed to always be taking her clothes off, which first started when we picked them up at the Dulles Airport. The next time we saw her, she was already three years old and still growing. Ted had taught her all the old songs and it was fun to hear her sing, "Red Sails in the Sunset". She and I had so much fun dancing together, and she loved dressing up and putting on all my wigs.

    Many years later, Virginia, Mary and Adrian came for another holiday to see us in Sleepy Hollow. We all decided to drive our minivan for a fun day to Baltimore. We were having such a good time that we decided to stay longer, so we had to put more money in the parking meter. But wait a minute-where was the van? Had we forgotten where we had parked it? What a

Miriam teaching little Virginia how to dance.

shock, no van.... it had been stolen! Oh no, bad timing. The police said they could not do anything and we were devastated. We hired a car to get home and it wasn't until three weeks later that our minivan had been found. When we picked it up and looked inside, we found a small children's book. The lovely carpet ceiling had been stripped and it was a mess. Guess they were looking for drugs. I have to admit, Baltimore left a bad taste in our mouths.

1982: Jack's Retirement
Around that same time period, Jack and his brother Albert were not seeing "eye to eye" on business issues. I did not know what to expect next. Shortly after that, and on a vacation trip back in Florida, Jack and I took a long walk on the beach and began discussing some very important life issues. I knew after almost forty years of hard work, and at sixty two years old, Jack was burnt out. I asked him, "Honey, do you need to make more money which will create more stress, or do you want a peaceful life with better health?" The answer was pretty obvious. I knew if we lived near the ocean we would extend our lives. So after a short vacation, we returned to Virginia.

In July of 1982, Jack sold his business to Albert. It was a big decision, but the right one. This was a very hard time for Jack. After all, he had started out on a shoestring and his business was his baby, but it was time to move on. We stayed on as consultants, but when you hand over the reins, new business owners just don't want to see your face anymore, and certainly don't want your advice. Along with the decision to sell the business, we also decided to sell our house in Sleepy Hollow, and move to Florida full time.

I wanted to sell our house furnished by October. We placed a great ad in the paper that read, "Buy a lifestyle, not a house" and sold it ourselves. It was a very special house, after all, it was the house that Jack and I built. But I was worried whether or not we could really sell it, and just walk away. But a nice couple bought it after many lookers, so I got my wish. It was a sad goodbye, and I never wanted to go back after that because of too many memories.

Jack and I had two sets of friends that we were very close to, and shared many good times. So when we sold our house and left Virginia, so did our friends. One moved to Pennsylvania, and the other couple to Texas. In later years, we all visited again. Good friends are very important and we certainly were blessed with many.

Moving to Florida Full-Time

When we moved to Florida we did not need to use a moving truck. We just took a few special things we treasured, and drove to Florida in our minivan. Joyce and Ted drove our big motor home and another friend followed behind in our Mercedes. It was so good to be able to share our condo with Joyce and Ted, and it meant a lot to Jack and me. We left Virginia after living there for 29 years, but I was worried Jack would be sad, because it held so many good times and friends. Would he really be as happy living in Florida? Time would tell.

The vacation condo we owned at the Racquet Club in Vero Beach Florida was already furnished, so we settled right in. No more cold winters, no more coping with the snow, and no more trying to drive on icy roads. Our condo in Florida was a fun place for vacations, but this was going to be very different. For 29 years we enjoyed living in a large private home and always a had project underway, but we adjusted.

Jack soon joined the Vero Beach Rotary Club. Around that same time we also met a super couple at a party in the clubhouse. He was a stockbroker and had an office in Vero. Jack was interested in the stock market and enjoyed managing his own stocks, with the help of advisors. I knew Jack was ready to get involved in something new, so he took his Series 7 Broker's Exam in Orlando. After many days of study, he passed and I was very proud of him. It was a tough exam, so tough that many younger people were there taking the exam over, some after several times. But we hadn't found out about his passing the test until we took a trip to California, to see our friend Dale who sponsored Jack for his Series 7 license. Dale and his wife took us to dinner and ordered champagne and said, "Here is a toast to my new business associate", what an exciting moment!

Jack went to work at Dale's office in Vero Beach, and would walk there most days since everything was very close in our little town. Having his license helped Jack build his own private stock portfolio. He was a very clever man and learned a lot about investing. In 1989, Jack invested his first three hundred dollars through a broker in Washington, which he had met in the past. Jack's new endeavors as a stock broker put us in an even better financial position. As the saying goes, "The future is yours". Just remember to seize new opportunities, and continue to make new friends often.

Disney World, USA

We loved Florida and all it had to offer, especially Disney World in Orlando. After mother and father were gone, the younger generation came for visits to America. Mary, Adrian and Virginia visited us and we took them to Disney World and Epcot on New Year's Eve. It was Virginia's first time and Mary and Adrian's second. What a great time we all had. Jack and I loved Disney and Epcot, and we made sure there wasn't any part of it that we missed. We have taken our family there many times, as there is so much to see. On this particular trip we rented a nice townhouse for all of us to stay and the weather was freezing, unlike anything we were familiar with in Florida. But that cold snap didn't hold us back. At midnight in Epcot all the lights came on and they played the national anthem for each country. When it came to England, we all shouted and sang at the top of our lungs, "Land of Hope and Glory, Mother of the Free". All of us were dancing to keep warm while smiling, laughing and celebrating our time together. It was a super night!

Going to Disney makes you feel like you are four years old again. While the Swan Hotel was our favorite place to stay because of its short walk to the Monorail, our first stay was at the Hawaiian Hotel on Disney property. I remember it was Christmas and this time it was warm. There was a Christmas parade at 3 pm on Main Street in the Magic Kingdom. To see all the excitement on the children's faces was truly magical, and I was just as excited as they were to see Mickey, Minnie and Donald Duck. Thank heaven for Disney, who opened up a whole new fantasy world. Think of all the pleasure that he has given to millions of people, and there are still millions more to come.

Disney memories are abundant in my mind. One time, my niece Lynn's children came for a visit and Jack and I booked two hotel rooms at the Swan, in Disney World. I think Tom was twenty and Frances eighteen. They went off and did their own thing, but didn't miss much. On one evening we decided to meet them at an English pub in Epcot. We arrived early and took an outside seat. An odd thing happened after we sat down. There was a window that looked into the pub from the outside, and all of a sudden we noticed an attractive lady playing the piano. She was the image of my sister Kathleen! After Tom and Frances arrived, they could not believe the likeness. She spotted us and stopped playing the piano, as if she was saying "How nice of you to give my grandchildren such a good time". We went inside and told her our story, even took her picture. It was just like Kathleen came back to life….so strange…I had cold chills and still do when I think of it. Now Tom and Frances have children of their own, and I hope one day they can take them to Disney to share all it has to offer. One year, Jack asked me what I wanted for Christmas and I said "Buy Disney stock for me". That was years ago and I will never sell it. Another smart move!

Chapter 14
1986: Our New Home in the Galleons

New Friends and More Pleasure

Florida was now our full time permanent residence. Soon after our move, we came to the realization that our condo at the Racquet Club was great for part time living, but we needed more room for a permanent lifestyle.

I happened to run into a friend of mine who was in the real estate business named Judy, a Realtor at the Moorings Yacht and Country Club. The Moorings was just south of the Racquet Club, but still in Vero Beach on the ocean. Judy said she would keep her eyes open for us, and it wasn't too long after that we received a phone call from her. She told us all about a condo she had just placed on the market. It was on the oceanfront in a subdivision called the Moorings, and in a condominium complex called "The Galleons". It had three bedrooms, three baths, three balconies, and a lovely living room with very high ceilings. Plus it was elegantly furnished! Jack and I had looked at this development before we bought at the Racquet Club, but said he didn't think we could afford it. It just so happened the owner was going broke because of his high life style, so we made an offer that I thought was too low. Oh my, how I wanted that as our new home!

During this particular timeframe of our offer, we had to make a trip back to Virginia to check on the motel. I asked Jack if he would please raise the offer so we would not miss out on purchasing the condo, so Jack called Judy back. On our drive back to Florida I was so anxious to find out what had happened, that I asked Jack to please phone Judy again. So we stopped at a rest area that had a phone booth and Jack made the call. Watching him walk back to the car had me concerned, as I could not tell what was going on. He opened the door and looked at me and said, "Honey, you have got yourself a condo at the Moorings". I was so happy!

Once back in Vero, we met first with the owner's wife. I was afraid the furnishings, especially the beautiful Venetian chandeliers, would not be ours. To our surprise, all they wanted was a picture of an Indian that dominated the living room wall. I could not have lived with Sitting Bull anyway, and found out it was on loan from a local gallery. They just wanted to keep a couple of lamps, a TV and some rugs - but that's it, everything else was ours.

We were in heaven with our new home. A very upscale company had done all the interior decorating, including a super parquet wood floor. No wonder the previous owner went broke. In October of 1986, you needed a country club membership for the Moorings Yacht and Country Club, in order to sell your condominium. The seller was going to have to give up his membership, hence the quick sale and our fantastic bargain. Separately we bought the club membership for twenty thousand dollars.

In February of that same year, we had rented the Racquet Club condo to a nice couple. When they knew we were about to sell it, they bought it fast, furniture and all. I also sold the minivan to a painter who was doing an odd job for us. Jack could not believe it, calling me "the forever salesman". The painter said he was looking for a van, so I said, "Come with me" and when he saw it he said "Sold"!

Once settled into the Galleons, we met the couple

that had bought the condo beneath us, which was unit #207, we were #307. They had made a higher bid on ours previously, but the owner thought he could get more money, so he turned them down. Betty and Mike were pleased for us, and we were all about the same age. I could not believe they had eight children, all great; and the boys were doctors like their father Mike. I asked him if he was catholic or a sex maniac, and he answered "both". We laughed and became best of friends.

Their winter home was on the water in Avalon, Pennsylvania and was fabulous. We stayed at their home later on, when their daughter Bonnie got married. Jack and Mike would play golf together and loved walking the beach, admiring all the girls. Betty and I loved bargain shopping and Jack and I loved their children, who spent a lot of time with us. Bruce, the eldest, had a doctor's practice in Ft. Lauderdale, just two hours away.

We also could not wait to show our new condo to our good friends Pat and Jack. I remember when they first came over and we were all sitting in the living room. Pat said, "I am expecting a moving van to pull in any minute and take everything away". She could not believe it was all ours and neither could we. Additionally, Jack was very pleased to have an office all to himself. He spent many hours working on his stocks and eventually gave up working as a stock broker. Jack now devoted himself to building our own stock portfolio, and that time spent really paid off.

Golf and Tennis

Jack also loved his golf and won many trophies. But it was the friendships he made that were more important to him. The Moorings Golf Club is such a lovely course overlooking the river, and it was a perfect place for our lifestyle. Tennis was my game, and I could even ride my bike to the courts, since it was all so close. I took many tennis lessons and joined the tennis team. We played at several other clubs, told more jokes and had more fun than I could have ever imagined. It was a wonderful group of people, and they always had a lot of parties.

The Round Robin in tennis was where you got to play with all ages, and I enjoyed that very much until I broke my wrist. That particular day Jack was playing golf. When he heard I was hurt, he rushed me to a special doctor that took care of me immediately. But, that wasn't going to slow me down; I even went to a dinner party that night with my arm in a sling. I remembered that you always hurt more the next day, so I decided to enjoy it while I could.

Jack lovingly took me to physical therapy three times a week, and waited while I had therapy on my wrist. He could not believe how I just mixed into conversations with some of the funniest people, from all walks of life, some not as fortunate as us. I told Jack, "It does not matter who they are, because they are all hurting just like I was." But I have to admit, I was pretty

My dearest friend, Marcy Von Kohorn and Miriam at the Galleons.

disappointed because I had to give up tennis due to my wrist. Oh how I missed my friends, but we all stayed in touch.

One person in particular named Marcy Von Kohorn, stood out the most. I dearly love her and her wonderful family. She is my very dearest friend and we have adopted each other. She is very special to me and always will be.

Planes & Boats - What Fun!

Now I must tell you about even more friends we met. John and Nell Menn lived at the Galleons, and had a winter home in Wisconsin. John was a lawyer and had big law firm. He was very clever man and hired many lawyers and ran a tight ship. He owned a six passenger plane and often liked Jack to co-pilot with him. They would call us on very short notice to fly to different places and we never said "no". I will never forget flying with them to a special dinner in Charleston South Carolina, where there was no prices on the menu. A fabulous opera singer entertained us during an incredible six course dinner. Oh what a night!

On another occasion, the six of us flew to the Bahamas, and Jack was on cloud nine as John let him fly the plane and land it safely on his own. What a great job! Jack became very fond of John and it worked both ways. Nell was a classic pianist; it was so great to hear her play. She was also a very pretty and elegant woman.

Another time the six of us flew to the Florida Keys, but the weather turned bad so the pilots decided we should stay the night in Key West, and fly back the next day. John was quite a character. He booked us into the hotel stating we were "Air Wisconsin" crew members. The oldest they had ever seen, I'm sure. We were not prepared for a layover, as we had no toothbrush, but at least we didn't have to decide what to wear the next day, ha!

The Galleons opened so many doors. We were a special group of people and it was a wonderful time in our lives. It was now the summer and we would soon be looking to travel somewhere to get out of the Florida heat, but not quite yet. You see, John also had a pontoon boat he kept docked at the marina close by where we lived. He named it "First Mistake". We used it more than he did, and he practically gave it to us. It was so much fun to take friends for a ride around the river and through the waterways of the Moorings, and gaze at the beautiful homes and elegant mansions. Jack was very good at handling the boat, as it was not easy getting it in and out of the dock at the Marina. Boating was so fun and we all enjoyed it!

John and Nell separated after fifty eight years of marriage. John had been living a double life with a Pan Am Stewardess named Crystal, who was from Germany. John had met her at a New York jewelry store, of all places. Nell was broken hearted and they divorced. John married Crystal and he kept the Galleons condo, and also bought Crystal an apartment in New York. She also had a family place in Germany. It took a while for us to adjust and accept Crystal, especially for Jack. She was a fun person and loved her champagne. She soon remodeled the condo to her liking, and in time, we all went out together.

One year a hurricane was on the path to Vero Beach, and in order to escape Jack booked a hotel in the Disney Resort properties called "The Swan" in Orlando, our favorite. We left a message on our home telephone that said, "Gone to see Mickey and Minnie". John and Crystal followed us, and once we arrived we saw many people trying to get prepared. The next morning the local newspaper showed a duck walking into the Magic Kingdom, as it was all deserted. Crystal and I later became good friends and she now lives in New York and Germany. John sold his plane and boat, because he was not well. He lost his zest for living I think, and donated many things to charity and unfortunately, Jack lost a good pal.

As you know, Jack and I loved to dance and we

were always looking for a place to go dancing. We found a super hotel about fifteen minutes south of in Vero, called the Radisson Hotel (which unfortunately is no longer there). Two fellows played the best music to dance to, and we went every Friday or Saturday night (and sometimes both). Our friends loved it as well, and Jack would always get the band to play his favorite song, "I Only Have Eyes for You". We would show off doing the Cha-Cha, which we learned long ago, taking dance lessons with Sylvia and Norman. Dance, dance, dance - that was me! There was this one couple that were friends of Joyce and Ted's that visited us. This couple danced competitively, and he was the best dancer I had seen. We took them to the Moorings Club, where he danced many dances with me. People stopped to watch while I was gliding across the floor on cloud nine. When an Englishman holds you close to dance, there is a big difference - forget the cheek to cheek stuff. English girls were not jitterbug dancers, and the Americans were the best. I loved to watch them, which is portrayed so well in old movies. Our life at the Galleons in the Moorings, and all the friends we made, brought many endearing moments to Jack and me. Whether it was dancing, socializing, golfing or tennis, we were meant to be together and so fortunate for all of our friends and family.

Chapter 15
Amazing Journeys

Puerto Rico & Acapulco

Carrol, our business partner in the motel in Virginia, owned two condominiums in Puerto Rico. He was very kind to let Jack and I take a holiday there. You could see the cruise ships from the balcony. We loved having our cocktails after five and watch all the different people through a telescope that Carroll had on his balcony. The beaches were beautiful, no matter which side of the island. I liked Puerto Rico beaches, because they often had a parade of people constantly coming by. We would sit on the sand and watch the locals stop by to try and sell us pineapple or coconut drinks. And some of the island women would hand make bikinis and other items to sell to the tourists. Truly interesting!

Puerto Rico night life was truly superb and such an exciting unique break in our life. We ended taking a second trip there for business, hosted by a company we bought supplies from. On that trip we took along another couple who were from Maryland and still exchange Christmas cards. But this time in Puerto Rico we had a bad experience. We decided to go to the casino, and while we were there our hotel room was robbed. Obviously this did not say much for their security.

On another evening while Jack was playing

Blackjack, I took a seat close by in a nice big comfortable chair. I did not care to gamble, but loved to people watch. Several men passed by and really gave me the eye. I was flattered, but did not think I looked that good. A girl in a very low cut dress approached me and said in no uncertain terms, "You are sitting in my chair!", in other words, get lost! I found out this was one of the chairs the local prostitutes parked themselves in. Ha - no wonder I was getting all that attention! Jack thought it was so funny and asked me how much I made. Of course, I just laughed.

When we were leaving Puerto Rico to catch a plane back to Washington, Jack lost his camera in the airport. A nice youth came running towards us with the camera, and Jack was so happy. He did not want to lose the all the pictures he had taken, plus the camera was very expensive. This just proved there are good and bad people in the world, and it left a nice taste of Puerto Rico for us and helped us forget the robbery.

Acapulco is also a truly magnificent place. It was so casual and we loved our vacation there. The incredible cliff divers would take that leap of faith off the cliffs, 136 feet into the Pacific Ocean. We could see why movie stars bought homes there, as it was very unique, beautiful, rugged and dramatic. How lucky and blessed we are to have so many vast experiences and be able to visit so many enchanting places. There are so many people who will never get that chance, so sad.

Our California Road Trip

In 1991 Jack and I decided to take a road trip to California in our minivan, and made numerous amazing stops. The entire trip was simply incredible. Along the way we listened to books on tapes and changed drivers as needed, and then included stops to see a few good friends. Margaret Spence was one of them, and lived in San Antonio Texas. What a shame she wasn't spending this time with Bob, as they could have been very happy together. You see, Bob took his own life. It was very distressing, as he shot himself and the horror was that Margaret found him. We were told about this on one of our return trips from England; such a terrible loss.

    We continued our drive through Tuscan, where the sun peeked through the mountains onto the large cactuses. We even saw a prairie dog, such a unique sight. Then on to Gila Bend, where the temperature rose to 109 degrees, humidity of 27. No wonder there was a sign that said, "Drive at Night, Sleep by Day". The sunset was one beautiful blaze as we settled into different motels along the way. And when the sun rose, the moon would still be shining; a spectacular show of beauty and support for our daily adventures. How lucky we were to see all of this with our own eyes. Finally making our way through New Mexico, we arrived in San Diego, and a beautiful 73 degrees. We met up with Pat and Jack, who had a super home overlooking the Polo Grounds. We spent a great evening with them at the Mazda Tennis Tournament - very nice.

    Now on to Laguna Beach, driving along the coast enthralled with the spectacular views. Then a quick stop at Dana Point for a yummy lunch, and oh yes, their homemade custard and bread pudding with whiskey sour sauce. Speaking of food, Coronado was next where the famous "Marie Callender's Restaurant and Bakery" was located, oh so good. It was also the place where the movie "Some like It Hot" was filmed. There just were so many sights to see, the excitement in the air was around every corner and filled every day.

    The next morning we attended a Polo Match, where lots of movie stars would go to take part of this hip and trendy sporting event. Later that same day we looked up and saw the evening air full of hot air balloons going up, up and away, and then landing close by. Hot Air Ballooning was a very popular local sport, and I could understand why they loved it so much. After all, the beauty of California was breathtaking. Goodness, our trip was so full; it made me think of the film, "Around the World in 80 days". Such happy times Jack and I were having, and oh so wonderful. So far, I thought San Diego had the most perfect climate; but we hadn't finished our trip. Paradise was everywhere, and Canyon Lakes was where Les and Barbara lived. To put you in the picture, Les was a man we had met on the Queen Elizabeth when he was traveling on his own, while his wife Barbara stayed longer in England. Les liked the ladies and knew he was fine looking, so I stayed close to Jack. Our stay was wrapping up, so we left and headed to Santa Barbara.

I just loved the incredible picturesque drives. There was not a postcard that could have been any better. We stopped at the Fess Parker Hotel, which boasts twenty-four acres right along the southern California coastline. Then, the famous Biltmore, a gracious oceanfront venue opened in 1927 and now a Four Seasons Resort. Smashing! Quaint and symbolic was the cute and tiny Danish town of Solvang. A darling place, full of bakeries and unusual buildings on cobblestone streets, lined with gas lanterns. Among many of our stops included Madonna's Inn, which featured a "think pink" centric approach, and themed guest rooms. Oh yes, and Jack thought it was great too, especially the men's room which was full of nude pictures.

The coastal drive to Monterey was quite a thrilling drive. This was to be a hundred and thirty mile trek between huge cliffs, the ocean and redwood trees. Stopping in San Francisco, we were in awe' with its magnificent Golden Gate Bridge, especially at night when all of its lights would brighten up the world. Close by was the charming little town of "Tiberon", which we fell in love with and stayed for several days. We would take the ferry back and forth to San Fran, which made it very convenient. Most people who worked downtown would commute back and forth using a motor bike to get around. How nifty. San Francisco is a near perfect place to visit. While the weather was cool and often foggy, people would come from all over the world seeking culture, outdoor adventures' and top-notch food and wine. As I sipped some of the best Irish coffee ever, we would ride the cable cars on Lombardi Street. It was all so unusually beautiful and a real must to experience. The fresh seafood at Fisherman's Wharf is marvelously delicious, and a real treat when mixed with the homemade San Francisco bread. And the nightlife is almost impossible to describe and intimately special. There was a super show of female impersonators, with the men in their wigs and perfect makeup and women's clothes. Many of them looked better than a lot of the females -ha. They loved impersonating movie stars, including Betty Davis, which was really amazing. Even the waiters serving cocktails were gay, and one said "Thank you sweetheart" to Jack when he gave him a tip. We had a royally good laugh. On our way through the capitol of Sacramento, we truly established an authentic understanding of what California is all about. Full of natural beauty, including lovely gardens and policeman in shorts and on bicycles. And the significant buildings all around were so impressive. But we couldn't stay long because we were very excited about what was ahead. Oh yes; Napa Valley!

Napa Valley was a short distance from Sacramento, and Jack and I couldn't wait to taste the different wines and take the spectacular tours that boasted amazing views. From the Mondavi Vineyard to Christian Brothers, to the Sutter House Vineyards whose gardens and gazebo gave Jack and I another opportunity to sip and enjoy. Then down the road to Sterling Vineyards and Glenn Ellen Winery for some Sebastian and Zinfandel. Jack loved his wines and became quite an expert. I could only manage drinking two wines at this vineyard. Many young people were around, and one couple asked how long Jack and I had been married. They said we made a handsome couple, which was almost a first and truly made our day. The only other time when Jack and I were complimented was during one of our trips to Disney. We were out one evening to see a show on "How to be a Millionaire" and Jack spilled the beans. People stood up and started shaking our hands. I didn't think it was too unusual - guess we looked pretty good together and had wonderful memories that showed after fifty years. Jack was not just a husband to me, but also a wonderful friend. We were so lucky to have each other.

As our trip continued, we now headed to Nevada. Lake Tahoe was our first stop and very stunning, as it sat on the border of California and Nevada. It boasts an incredible freshwater lake and located sixty two hundred feet above sea level in the glorious Sierra Nevada Mountains. The giant trees and huge boulders adorn their incredibly blue lake, which would often change its blue hues to shades of aqua. The local town was my favorite called "Incline Village", located on the north side of Lake Tahoe, and encompasses a night life of gambling at the Hyatt Hotel. Such fun! Nearby was Carson City and Virginia City, old local western towns known for gold mining back in their day. Those small historic mining towns had to be the place where all the old cowboy movies were filmed, and of course now, set back behind the highways as tourist attractions. But this same route was also part of the Pony Express Trail back in 1860. So as part of history, we took that same trail to Reno Nevada, just fifty miles from Lake Tahoe. Besides gambling, Reno also offered great food and super entertainment. We even saw the show "Heavenly Bodies" which was terrific and very glamorous. Part of the performance included a mime comic that came from the London Palladian, and a mannequin number that displayed great imagination. The next day we saw a wonderful auto museum at Harrah's which displayed all the cars ever built in America, and poor Jack was sad not to see his first Chevrolet Nomad automobile up there, which first came to the market in 1956.

Amazed with our road trip to date, we shook our heads in astonishment of all the natural beauty, and still had more to see. Next was Salt Lake City. Once we arrived, we went to see the Mormon Tabernacle Temple which was completed in 1875. Close by the Temple was the Mormon Office building, and the view from the 26th floor observation deck was staggering. Brigham Young was one of the early proponents of Mormonism and a colonizer in Utah. They said he had up to fifty seven wives and fifty five children; poor guy……I mean, poor women! We also saw the Tabernacle Choir rehearsing. What a treat to see all different ages dedicated to expressing themselves through singing; you could just tell they loved it.

Colorado, here we come! We drove three hundred miles straight, and arrived in the heart of Vail, an upscale village in the Colorado Rockies well known for snow skiing and other outdoor activities. Vail was complete with little chalets everywhere, surrounded by colorful flowers and small bridges, with clear spring water flowing across the land. There was a free shuttle every few minutes that would take you to any point of interest, and every time we took a ride, the bus was always full of laughter and happy holiday makers. We ended our busy day at a good piano bar with a fireplace blazing away. It was so warm and cozy; we just hated to move on, but we knew tomorrow would bring even more wonderful memories for Jack and I. But Bear Lake was calling us, which had good music and a cobblestone square, famous for its unusual statues. And Colorado Springs is known as "The Gardens of God". Both are pretty awesome towns scattered with huge rocks, budding flowers and shade trees all around - just amazing! What an incredible vacation packed with all the beauty of America. I loved our trip. This road trip will always remain one of my most wonderful memories with Jack, which was completely filled with very, very happy times and totally amazing sites.

Maine & Canada

In August of 1997, while living at the Galleons, we had planned a trip to Virginia and rented a townhouse in Maine. A couple owned it who lived at the Moorings in the same subdivision where we lived. Just before we left, we heard the tragic news of Diana, the Princess of

Whales death in Paris, and how the whole world was in shock. After we checked the motel in Virginia, we stopped to visit some friends at the British Embassy in Washington. It was unbelievable to see all the hundreds of flower bouquets in her honor. So sad. She was so loved and remembered. We all felt for her two boys and for the loss of their beautiful young mother.

We continued our drive to Maine, and the place where we stayed was very elegant. We spent a week sightseeing and the local marina was close by, filled with expensive yachts. But after a couple of days, I became restless and wanted something more exciting to do. Jack informed me that Quebec, Canada was only five hours away. "Let's go" I said. Once there we found a nice hotel. What an exciting city! Jack went to the local Rotary for lunch and a nice fellow helped him with the language. I was happy to walk around and see the beautiful gardens. The restaurants were neat too, as the waiters encouraged tourists to come inside to taste the delicious specials on the menu. Canada is so old and historical and much to see, plus the people are especially kind. We then made our way to see Irene and Lee's family in Toronto. But on our way through customs, they stopped us to search our van. Apparently, we were in the duty free shop a long time before we crossed the border, deciding what wines to take to our friends. Imagine two golden oldies smuggling dope or something. They asked Jack if he had a weapon. He was getting mad, so he showed them a knife he always carried. They were amused and sent us on our way, wishing us a good trip. We had to laugh. We liked the big city in Toronto. There was so much to see, very different than when we visited Irene and Lee when they lived at North Bay. However, I do remember North Bay having the best fish and chips ever, second to England. Boy, what I wouldn't give for some right now!

After our trip to Canada, we stopped in New York. I wanted to see a Broadway show and we were able to score front row seats to the musical "Can-Can". Wow, it was very risqué, especially the can-can dancers.

Then after a little shopping, we headed home.

Miriam in her mink.

Chapter 16
The Rotary Club

I have mentioned Jack's involvement with the Rotary Club several times, as it was a big part of our lives. Many people in the Rotary were significantly dedicated, like Jack, so I wanted to tell you more about it.

The Rotary Club is the second largest non-governmental, non-religious service organization in the world, and has over a million Rotarians. They were originally known to be an all man's club, but in 1989 they started to include women. I was not pleased with that because it never seemed the same. Why do women have to get in the act all the time? It was different in England, because the women had their own club called "RotaryAnns", but I am not sure if that has changed now. I think some women who joined the Rotary worked hard to become the President of their local organization, but some just hoped to find a man instead.

I am amazed when I think of how the Rotary originally started. It was just a few businessmen sharing ideas, and now they have clubs all over the world. It is wonderful how many significant friendships were made. When you had a meeting in another part of the world, you exchanged clubs flags and developed new friends. I have to admit that what the Rotary stands for shows in everything they do, and supports their charter, "Service before Self".

One year while attending a Rotary Convention in Canada, we stayed in our motor home with many Rotarian's, who were all doing the same thing. The Rotary organization played a big part of our lives and we enjoyed all that it represented.

The Rotary Club of Virginia

Every year in February, we hosted the Rotary governors from all over the world. It would be a fun week in Virginia, before attending a convention and working session in California. They were thrilled to come to Virginia, especially because it was so close to Washington, the Capitol and all the historical sites. One evening while the Rotary governors were in town, we hosted a BBQ at the Rotarian house. Different couples would entertain them during the day, sightseeing, shopping and boat rides. Jack gave a wonderful tour of Washington, having lived there in his youth, which of course made him the most familiar.

We had many couples stay with us over the years, and in return we visited several in England. One couple in particular stood out in our memory, which made us feel very smug about the home we lived in. What a shock we had when they met us at the end of their long lovely driveway. Their house dated back to Oliver Cromwell, and was a huge sprawling estate. Talk about the Lord and Lady of the Manor! The only snag was our bedroom overlooked many fruit trees, and there were no screens on the windows. This enabled flies to make themselves at home inside our bedroom, and all over the walls and ceilings. Poor Jack, I made him kill those bugs with tissues making sure not to leave any marks. It sure taught us a lesson. No more bragging!

Vero Beach Rotary

Back in Vero Beach, Jack had a Rotary luncheon to attend at a nice hotel on the beach. They were all such a nice group of businessmen, no matter what country or state we visited. We were fortunate to be a part of such a great organization. We met Hannelore and Frank through the Rotary Club, and they had a condo next to the Galleons where we lived called "Sabal Reef". Frank had been a Pan American pilot and now retired. He also owned a small plane and loved to take his friends for a ride. Hannelore was a wonderful cook and was from Austria. We were invited to many dinner parties, and they had some very interesting friends from different countries we enjoyed meeting.

    Jack and I were also very active in fund raising, both in Virginia and Florida. I remember one idea Jack came up with to make money for charity while in Virginia having to do with making pancakes. I can just see him now in my convertible, with a woman dressed up as Aunt Jemima. The Rotary men would cook the pancakes and compete to see who could make the biggest stack. The event raised a lot of money that went to the needy.

    Jack became President of the Rotary Club in Vero Beach (as he did in Virginia), and every year the Governors would book a fun week in Florida. It would include one day at Disney's Epcot, in Orlando. The Rotary would hire a local bus from a Rotary member who owned a doughnut business, so he would supply the breakfast. I would get them all singing on the bus, and considering they were from different countries, it went pretty well. We only had trouble with one man who was from England, who asked early on where the pub was. We did find one at Epcot, and later bought everyone giant beers. It took three of us to keep track of everyone once we arrived. And one person in a wheel chair enabled us to get into places first, a real time saver. After a very tiring yet wonderful day, we all went to a fine hotel for drinks and dinner. The next morning we would drive back to Vero Beach to end a great week.

    One time when Jack flew to Switzerland for a Rotary meeting. He wasn't exactly sure where the meeting luncheon was located, so he asked a man on the street. Such luck, that man was also a Rotarian and was on his way to the same luncheon, and asked Jack to join him. I was not left alone during that time, as we had traveled to Switzerland with Lee and Irene. When Jack returned from his luncheon, he was very excited about how royally he was treated. He certainly deserved the recognition.

International Rotary Convention – France
    The International Rotary Conventions were always superb. There was another one in France, and I told Jack I particularly wanted see the French Riviera. Although Jack was not feeling very well, he decided we would go. The Rotarians went all out for us, making sure we had a nice hotel. We would all get together at night in the courtyard and have cocktails, tell stories and enjoy the diversity of everyone from different countries. I admire the French for a lot of their ways, especially their food, which was so good. I enjoyed the small portions, unlike the American meals that are too large and overpowering. To me, smaller was better.
    One night, they had a big parade down Main Street and we were in a café having drinks, a perfect spot to see it all. There were not enough chairs for everyone to sit down, so the owner went home and brought more from his own home for people to sit and enjoy. How nice can you be? You have not lived until you attend an International Rotary Convention. We did a lot of sightseeing while there, including Monte Carlo. The beaches were lovely and all the women were topless. The men thought it was great to see so many beautiful women, but I thought the French girls were not very well endowed.
    While in Paris we saw a lot of topless shows, but the women were not allowed to move around much on stage. It reminded me of when we last saw father in a special show in England. He was backstage smoking with several nude ladies. The "NUDE Crackers" came to England - ha! Once more Jack's eyes almost popped out of his head. Then there was the famous Windmill

Theatre, which I still have a program from that I treasure. I have to admit, the nudes were so lovely. It was well presented in the great movie "Mrs. Henderson Presents", which is a true story. Back then the shows were nonstop, and the theater never closed all through the war. It meant so much for the servicemen to forget the war, even for a brief time, no matter who was performing. We had happy memories of Paris, and the night clubs served endless champagne, all part of the cover charge.

One evening while still in France, Jack had a little too much to drink. I knew I had to get him back to the hotel, and took him on the Metro Rail system. Why I didn't get a taxi I will never know, but we made it. While in Paris, Jack took me out and we were walking the streets when two men passed by and said to each other "expensive". We had to laugh, if you know what I mean. And if you wanted to go to the rest room in Paris, be ready to see a man trimming his beard. Yes, there were no Ladies and Gentleman restrooms. Everyone shared the same one, but at least it was free. In England they use to charge to use a public restroom, and sure enough, when you needed to use the facility you never had the right change.

Let's get back to Jack. Through our trip, Jack continued to feel bad and started to have a lot of pain. We ended up going to see both a French and English doctor, but no help. He couldn't wait to get back to the United States to see his own doctor in Vero Beach, who immediately put him on Prednisone. This was a new doctor for Jack. I thought to myself, "I wished we had seen this doctor in the past". The other doctors Jack had previously seen, had given him the wrong treatments for his ailments. Jack about kissed the ground when we landed. What a trooper!

Chapter 17
The Love I Hold in My Heart

My Mother

I have talked a lot about my family in this book, but the one I loved the most I have not talked about much and that is my beloved mother Sarah, but called Sally. Sally was from a big family of thirteen, which was not unusual in her day. Some of her family went to find a new life in Canada, and only came back to visit once or twice. Mother had one sister named Ethel, who was the youngest and I remember her the most. Ethel was in love with a married man and while she did marry someone else, she was very unhappy. She had a lovely home outside of Nottingham and when I was about ten years old, Joyce and I would go to stay with her on occasion. Ethel loved the Opera, but always played the sad songs. One day while I was at home, mother sent me to my room for no apparent reason. My aunt had just arrived to see my mother, and privately told her some frightening news. Her sister Ethel had taken her own life by swallowing poison. She was only twenty eight years old - what a terrible waste. I remember her being so kind to Joyce and me and was very petite and pretty. I was too young to know just how my mother felt, but she eventually told me the news when I was older.

Mother also had a brother that lost both his legs

early in life, and another brother who was very smart and invented many things, and another she lost in the war. In big families children often grow apart, and that sure was obvious for my poor mother. A very special and a pretty woman, my mother had long blonde hair, natural for those days (which was rare), and it flowed all the way down her back. She was alone much of the time because father was out entertaining. But she never complained and was happy to be a homemaker. It meant so much to me to get home from school and see mother there waiting for me. We also had a nanny when I was young, because mother had some health problems - but nothing serious.

I was a handful at an early age and very independent. I was caught swearing occasionally and Joyce would run and tell on me, but she also said "Mom please don't hit her". I have to laugh about it now. One time Joyce was invited to a children's party and the lady hosting it told her, "Have Miriam come later because she upsets things". When I heard that, I went up to the woman and said "Keep your bloody party!" and everyone was in shock. They could not believe these words could come from someone so young and pretty. Even at four I was so self-sufficient, that I didn't even want my mother back stage to help me get ready to perform. I never heard my mother or father swear, so it is amazing how children pick up things. There is a saying, "There was a little girl, who had a little curl, right in the middle of her forward, and when she was good she was very, very good, but when she was bad she was horrid"; well I guess that was me -Miriam.

My mother had the most wonderful sayings and was a wit at Proverbs. She loved to read and was great at Shakespeare. She told me you really have a friend when you have a book to read, so true. In later years, when she lived with Jack and me in Virginia, I would go into her bedroom to check up on her. I would always find her asleep with a book in her hand; such a dear lady and a true class act. I miss her so often.

There are so many things you wish you could ask your parents once they are gone. Both my mother and father were down-to-earth people; their generation was truly an inspiration. I feel sorry for the children who grow up with single parents, and while I never knew my grandparents, I feel I missed a lot. Older people have so much to offer and share. Younger people should take the time to hear their stories, learn from them and ask more questions. Having lost my two sisters, I feel blessed their children are so close to me now. There is a lot of shared love with my nieces and their children. I am also very fond of Susan, Jack's niece and family, as well as my dear Mark in California. Jack had a lot of health problems that we got through together, and at the end, it was not easy. It never is.

My Forever Jack

I thank heaven for the wonderful years Jack and I shared. He was not just a husband, he was my dearest friend, caring, loving and always there for me. I could not begin to describe our life together, as we were so well matched. Jack went to college in Virginia and graduated from UVA in Charlottesville. He drove a "Good Humor" ice cream truck to make a little extra money and gave the reject ice cream to the poor children.

Jack joined the Air Force and became a pilot. He crashed a small plane while training, but was not badly hurt, and the Air Force made him fly again right away so he would not lose his nerve. He said it was a wonderful day when he earned his wings and he was so proud; rightly so! He had a great sense of humor, and I was the lucky one because he loved British shows like "One Foot in The Grave", "Faulty Towers" and "Vicar of Dibley". We watched them all together numerous times. But the movie he loved the most and we watched together often was "Brief Encounter", how apropos.

In later years he spent a lot of time on the computer, building up his stock portfolio, which he was very good at due to his wonderful mind. Jack also had an artistic flair and could make all kinds of creative cards and party invitations, homemade birthday cards and anniversary cards, you name it. But the cards he made for me were the most special.

Our best times ever are when Jack and I spent them together, just the two of us alone. We loved the beach; he loved to fish and golf. Jack was a Libra, equally paring with my personality as a Gemini. He had a way of always smoothing my feathers, if I became fluttered. Jack passed away in April of 2009, after being very ill. We had a good doctor named Dr. Kanzler who helped as much as he could, but regardless, the end was very difficult and sad. I was his caregiver for over two years while he was on dialysis. It was very hard. Bless my Jack. He even found the strength to have a nurse order two dozen roses for me. I can see him now sitting in the chair in the dining room, watching the door for the delivery man. It was Valentine's Day and when I saw the roses I could not help but cry. I was the love of his life, as he was mine.

Being left alone now is very tough, but you find the strength somehow to carry on. So many people are in the same boat. Now dear friends, please know that YOU are a blessing. Keep cheerful, no one wants misery around. Yes, you will miss many things, no man to hold you in his arms, to tell you how nice you look, sharing your life to wake up together in the morning, seeing that dear face and ready to share another beautiful day with just you. Someone to tell your troubles to, one that understands you and treasures you just the way you are. Love is everything in life, and you are so blessed to have it.

Mary, my dearest niece is like a daughter to me and we are very close. I know she truly loves me. Both Lynn and Mary have lovely children and grandchildren and I am very happy for them. I am sorry we did not have any children. I believe I was meant to be a second mother and share in their lives, and I love it when they visit me. As I come to the end of my story, I must tell

you why I chose the title "One In A Million". You see, one million Americans came to England in World War II, and I was lucky enough to capture the heart of that one in a million. I feel Jack is waiting for me, we never really parted.
Thanks for the memories.
Miriam

Afterword

I received this letter after finishing my book and thought it was so sweet, I wanted to include it. What a perfect opportunity to use it as a softhearted afterword, which I now have happily been able to get finished and in your hands.

My Auntie Miriam

My Auntie Miriam left England for a life in America shortly after I was born. It was a momentous and very brave decision to make for one so young. It meant leaving her homeland and all of her family (which now included me) and putting her eggs all in one basket, so to speak. The basket in question was called "Jack". In hindsight it proved to be a very wise decision. For me it seemed to be a very romantic decision, which made Auntie Miriam very different than my three other Aunties. I now had a glamorous, adventurous relative living a life I could only dream of which would fascinate me for years to come. It would have been understandable if Miriam had given little thought to me. This however, was not the case. There were numerous gifts sent from America. My first walking doll, with hair I could brush, a baby doll with soft arms and legs, so life like. Indian boots, a cross between a sock and a slipper-nothing like them in England. A lovely blue zip up jacket that I loved to flaunt in front of my friends and say, "My Auntie Miriam sent this to me all the way from America". I remember all of these gifts and more so vividly.

My Auntie and Uncle Jack (a larger than life character), would come to visit from time to time and brought their fantastic American car with them. It was two-toned, long and sleek with beautiful leather seats. My family did not have a car so you can imagine how impressed I was. They took us to Skegness England in it and I sat next to Jack in the front seat. Everyone starred at us and I felt like royalty.

In between their visits there were photographs and letters and occasionally a cinema film with Jack and Miriam talking to us, and showing us their lovely home. All the family, Mum, Dad, John, Me, Uncle Ted, Auntie Joyce and my cousin Mary would all gather together at Grandma and Grandpa's house to watch these films. It was a really good family get together. We would eat, drink and talk and it seemed like Uncle Jack and Auntie Miriam were there as well.

My grandma and grandpa must have missed her terribly, but were lucky enough to make the trip to America, more than on one occasion. Also, my Uncle and Auntie and their daughter Mary were able to make a visit. My parents never went. So sad, neither did John or I, until later in life. She traveled, went to parties, swam, played tennis, and entertained many friends at her home and so on.

As the years past we kept in touch through photographs and letters. I always wanted to go to America to see my Aunt and Uncle and their lovely home, and taste a little of their lifestyle, but it never seemed to be possible. When Miriam and Jack came to visit us in Shropshire, I realized just how much I was missing and was determined to one day get there.

Miriam and Jack spent a lot of money and energy on my two youngest children, Tom and Frances, and treated them to a trip to America. This was an opportunity for my children to experience something near and dear to my heart, something I never got a chance to. They had a wonderful time, which made me want to go even more. They even took them to Disneyworld, which they so loved.

When my children had grown up and left home, both my mother and mother in law had passed away. I decided it was time to treat ourselves to our first trip to America. We only had one week, but it was lovely. Jack and Miriam had met us at the airport, and Jack drove us to his home in his big van, six seats and even a television. Outside their front door was a big banner with our names on it. What a welcome!! We had a glorious week! Jack would never let us pay for anything and they took us to Palm Beach, Epcot, dinner at the club and numerous other restaurants. Miriam wanted to buy me clothes and still does....bless her.

So we started our love affair with Vero Beach, and I rekindled my relationship with my favorite Aunt. I regret all those years that I didn't get to see her. But now every time I do see her, it is even more special. Now when my husband Barry and I pay a visit to Miriam, we instantly feel at home. Miriam is my Aunt, my second mother, my sister and my friend. She makes me feel loved and little things mean so much. It could be as small as a squeeze on my wrist by her hand, or watching television together or having fun trying on clothes. Or sitting on the boardwalk quietly talking about the past and our family, or how much she misses me when I leave. All these things are important to me and I value them immensely. I don't like when I have to leave her and I would love to stay longer or visit more often.

I know life isn't easy now for Miriam, as she is always in pain, and I would love to be there for her. However, whatever Miriam is, she is no shrinking violet. Despite her diminutive size, she is a plucky fighter and does not give in easily. She is pretty remarkable despite all of the trauma she has faced in the last few years. Her eyesight is better than mine and she walks easily and confidently, without any aids whatsoever. She has many very good friends, is popular and entertaining and may she continue to be so for many years to follow.

Miriam is my last contact with my parents and grandparents and I see my family traits in her which I find endearing. I love to hear her stories about the past, she has a rich and fascinating history that I am still hearing about, and I can't wait for the book. My mother was very proud of Miriam, yet somewhat envious of her life - which was so different than her own. She would show everyone pictures of her pretty, glamorous sister and admired her for being so fit, active and slim. As I grow older, I can see the genetic links that bind you to a family, certain physical attributes, characteristics and mannerisms. Miriam and I may be different ages, we may have led vastly different lives and made many different choices - but we have a unique bond. And even though we have not spent an awful lot of time together, I get the overriding impression that there is something that makes us very special to each other, and different from everyone else. It's a family thing. But sadly not everyone appreciates it, and if not careful they can lose it. It took a long time for me to get to know Miriam properly. She has always been there in my life and I have always loved her. Even from a distance I have come to know and appreciate how important she is to me, and what a lovely person she really is.

It takes a pretty strong character to do what Auntie Miriam did after the war. Jack recognized this and so do I. It paid off – she had a great life with Jack, which opened the door to America for us, and others from her family in England. Thank you Miriam for that. I look forward to many more visits with my special Auntie Miriam, so hang in there. I hope this letter is not too sloppy and sentimental, but it needed to be said.

Lots of Love as Always, Marilyn xx

Marilyn Genner is Miriam's niece, Kathleen's daughter, and lives in Devon England.

www.ingramcontent.com/pod-product-compliance
Lightning Source LLC
Chambersburg PA
CBHW040322300426
44112CB00020B/2842